Texas State Parks and the CCC

A|M travel guides

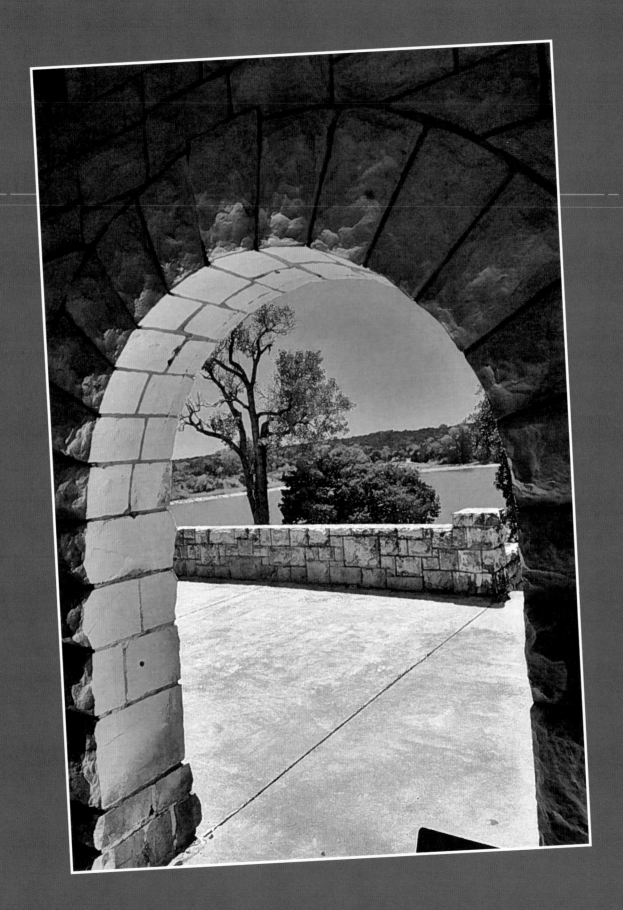

Texas State Parks and the CCC

The Legacy of the Civilian Conservation Corps

Cynthia Brandimarte *with* Angela Reed

Foreword by CARTER SMITH

Texas A&M University Press   *College Station*

Copyright ©2013 by Texas Parks and Wildlife Department
Manufactured in China by Everbest Printing Co.,
through FCI Print Group
First edition

This paper meets the requirements of
ANSI/NISO, Z39.48-1992
(Permanence of Paper).
Binding materials have been
chosen for durability.

Library of Congress Cataloging-in-Publication Data

Brandimarte, Cynthia A.
   Texas state parks and the CCC : the legacy of the Civilian
Conservation Corps / Cynthia Brandimarte with Angela Reed ;
foreword by Carter Smith. — 1st ed.
        p. cm.
   "Copyright © 2013 by Texas Parks and Wildlife Department—
ECIP t.p. verso.
   Texas A&M travel guides.
   Includes bibliographical references and index.
   ISBN-13: 978-1-60344-819-2 (flex : alk. paper)
   ISBN-10: 1-60344-819-5 (flex : alk. paper)
   ISBN-13: 978-1-60344-825-3 (e-book)
   ISBN-10: 1-60344-825-X (e-book)
   1. Parks—Texas—History—20th century.   2. Parks—Texas—
History—21st century.   3. Civilian Conservation Corps (U.S.)—
Texas—History.   I. Reed, Angela (Angela S.)   II. Texas. Parks
and Wildlife Dept.   III. Title.
   SB482.T4B73   2013
   333.78ʾ309764—dc23
   2012019926

Design: Barbara Haines

Funding from the
Texas Parks and Wildlife Department
helped make this book possible.

Frontispiece:

Designed by architects Olin Smith and John W. Wilder and built by the
men in CCC Company 1827 (V), the refectory arch frames a sunny view of
Meridian State Park. In addition to the refectory's impressive stone work,
the company constructed the dam on Bee Creek in order to form 70-acre
Meridian Lake. (Photo by Stan A. Williams, 2005, TxDOT)

For

Doug S. Porter Jr.

Thanks for keeping the CCC legacy alive.

CONTENTS

FOREWORD

The late state representative W. R. Chambers got it right. As he wryly noted to the *Dallas Morning News* in a comment on the makings behind a viable state park, "It requires more than a cow pasture and an excited chamber of commerce to make a park go." A whole lot more.

Be assured that the history of the Texas state park system is as scintillating and varied as the history contained within the grounds of the parks themselves. Tales of swashbuckling and double-crossing politicians, grueling political battles, eleventh-hour land saves, go-for-broke land deals, extraordinary feats of civic pride, boundless displays of generosity from citizens across the state, and more recently, devastating fits of nature, abound throughout the system.

Suffice it to say, the hands and will of many have joined Mother Nature in shaping the ninety-six-some-odd state parks that Texas families enjoy and cherish today. Individuals like former governor Pat Neff, who is largely credited for creating the state parks system, had the vision and persistence for making it happen way back when, in 1923. Legendary First Lady, Lady Bird Johnson never blinked when she was called upon to step in and save her beloved Enchanted Rock from its likely fate as a rock quarry. Senator Don Kennard sacrificed his own political career in order to devise an early funding stream, a penny tax on cigarettes, to support the parks. And over the last decade, tireless parks apologist and businessman George Bristol has led an unrelenting effort to keep parks at the fore of public consciousness and political discourse.

Their efforts have all been nothing short of Herculean. God bless 'em.

Yet another band of Texans, less known and certainly less fêted than the leaders mentioned above, also deserves our collective thanks and shouts of praise. This group hailed from the time of Tom Brokaw's "Greatest Generation," a coterie of young men: strong, fit, and able, oftentimes right off the farm, all struggling to find their way and establish their means during the depths of a depression like no other.

In the absence of any other meaningful job opportunity, these men, ages 18–25, enrolled in a Roosevelt-era public works program that was part military boot camp, part public service assignment, and part jobs training initiative. The program was the fabled Civilian Conservation Corps (CCC), which ultimately hosted over three million young men who literally and figuratively built hundreds of parks from the ground up. Say or think what you will about government sponsored jobs programs, but the young men of the CCC camps made a lasting and profound difference across our national and state parks like nobody before or after them ever has or likely ever will.

I could not be more proud of my Texas Parks and Wildlife colleague, Cynthia Brandimarte, and former CCC Legacy Parks coordinator Angela Reed, for so eloquently and creatively sharing the stories of the Texas-based CCC camps in their signature opus, *Texas State Parks and the CCC: The Legacy of the Civilian Conservation Corps.* Their work is a literal can't-miss for all who use and enjoy our state park system. As you read through their words and pore over the accompanying photos, you can't help but be spirited back in time to an unparalleled era of sacrifice and service that made the system, at least in large part, what it is today.

Better still, if you follow up your read with an excursion into any of the twenty-nine Texas state parks that hosted a CCC camp in the 1930s and early 1940s, you'll find their handiwork everywhere you turn: elaborately crafted refectories carved out of native stone, hand-hewn log cabins nestled just so under the sprawling canopies of a towering pine or hardwood, stone bridges spanning an otherwise impassible watercourse, custom-built rock overlooks atop a scenic hill or ridge, picturesque lakes made possible by hand-built dams, and much, much more.

The materials for these things were the stuff around them: rocks and stone, logs and timber. Their palette was the parks themselves. And work the CCC men did: from sunup to sundown, busily building bridges, roads, entries, lakes, trails, cabins, and meeting halls, all so that people from generations then and to come could enjoy the beauty, majesty, and wildness of the special places we know as our home ground.

I had my first exposure to the CCC craftsmen as a wide-eyed, elementary school kid on a late summer trip up into the Davis Mountains. It was my inaugural visit to West Texas, and I remember being mesmerized as we drove through the state park and headed up to the imposing pueblo structure known by all as Indian Lodge. The thick adobe walls and heavy timbered beams were what I thought a "mountain lodge" ought to look like. I'll never forget looking out the window on our first morning in the lodge and watching a mule deer doe with twin fawns easing down the mountain, with a small band of javelinas feeding off in the distance.

The only thing that would have made it better would have been the presence of Indian Lodge restaurant's famed namesake, a black bear!

Since that time, I have been blessed to visit many of the CCC-era parks. Among other things, I've swam in the pools at Abilene and Balmorhea, fished at Brownwood, paddled around the cypress knobs at Caddo Lake, danced on the "floor" at Garner, launched boats from Goose Island, traipsed through the woods at Palmetto, camped below the stars at Palo Duro Canyon, admired the Leon River bottomlands at Mother Neff, spent the night in the cabins of Bastrop, reflected on Texas battles and Spanish missionaries at Goliad, and hiked through the pines at Tyler. In short, thanks to the men of the CCC, I've had a grand ole time.

Texas state parks tell the life, history, and story of our great state. As Cindy and Angela so well attest, the CCC men played no small part in making that happen. As one of the many stewards at TPWD of this proud and vibrant heritage, I hope all of you will find time to walk through our history in some of the state's greatest treasures ever conceived, your state park system.

Carter P. Smith
Executive Director,
Texas Parks and Wildlife Commission
August 12, 2012

PREFACE

The story of the Civilian Conservation Corps (CCC) and how it built state parks in Texas between 1933 and 1942 needs to be told for those who steward the parks, the millions of Texans and others who visit them each year, the communities where the parks are located, and descendants of CCC workers who toiled so hard to build an important part of modern Texas.

The CCC was one of several large projects launched by the federal government during the Great Depression. The famous and far-reaching Works Progress Administration (WPA) overshadowed the CCC, as did some other initiatives of President Franklin D. Roosevelt's New Deal administration. The CCC was at first not a separate federal agency; it had to borrow its staff from the Departments of Agriculture, War, Interior (notably the National Park Service), and Labor, and even the US Office of Education. Nor was the CCC's launch marked by an attention-getting Washington ceremony; Roosevelt merely sketched his idea for a CCC and how it might be organized on a scrap of paper. And later there were slurs and snickers about the CCC's alleged inefficiencies. Indeed, if the men who worked so hard in the CCC had known they would one day be subjects of studies touting their historical uniqueness and importance, they would have found it hard to believe. They saw themselves, not inaccurately, as a ragtag lot dressed in ill-fitting army uniforms that, like the knapsacks on their backs, were leftovers from World War I. Yet the CCC became a cornerstone of the New Deal.

Given the CCC's relatively short duration, why is its story important? Nationally, between 2.5 and 3 million men joined the CCC, and 50,000 of them worked in Texas. Thousands of others were employed by the CCC to support its workers.[1]

Overwhelmingly, CCC enrollees came from families subsisting on relief benefits, and many found themselves far from home for the first time in their lives. Their children and grandchildren, nieces and nephews, spouses and colleagues have heard their personal stories, pored over their prized photo albums, and visited the parks and structures they built. When residents of Austin picnic at Zilker Park or those of Dallas go to White Rock Lake, when Texans vacation at Palo Duro Canyon State Park, or when visitors to Texas head straight to Big Bend National Park, they testify to the CCC's importance and its story's continued relevance.

This book recaptures, updates, and extends the CCC story for the benefit of Texans and others, reminding everyone of the debt owed to administrators, designers, and workers for their lasting contributions. Chapter 1 begins by recounting the circumstances that led to the CCC's creation and how it proved to be a watershed for building a Texas state park system, following mostly unsuccessful efforts to do so during the 1920s. Using CCC workers' own words and recollections, Chapter 2 describes typical experiences and lives of workers in Texas CCC camps. Chapter 3 assesses how the parks they built fared after the CCC was disbanded in 1942 until its fiftieth anniversary in 1983. Chapter 4 shows how Texas' rich legacy of CCC parks has been maintained and ponders how it can be sustained and enriched in coming years. An epilogue tells how, due to high temperatures and low rainfall during 2011, Texas almost lost many sturdy CCC buildings and features. Our aim is to expand readers' knowledge of the parks, encourage them to unearth new information about CCC features in them, and, most of all, visit and appreciate this precious and distinctive heritage.

ACKNOWLEDGMENTS

This illustrated publication is the culmination of many years' effort by those at Texas Parks and Wildlife Department (TPWD) who work as historians, architects, superintendents, archivists, curators, rangers, interpreters, artists, archeologists, resource managers, and general CCC enthusiasts, along with agency contractors and Texas students and scholars. The generosity of the Hillcrest Foundation, founded by Mrs. W. W. Caruth Sr., Dallas; the National Endowment for the Arts; and the Roy and Christine Sturgis Charitable and Educational Trust, Dallas, has continued to bear fruit for the study of the CCC, and as all good philanthropy does, it has opened learning possibilities for people.

This volume was initially conceived as a companion to the TPWD Web site *The Look of Nature: Designing Texas State Parks during the Great Depression*, and we are pleased to thank Doug Porter and Dennis Gerow of TPWD for ably assisting with its content. The Web site's principal historical advisers, James Wright Steely and Dan K. Utley, also deserve recognition because it was their pioneering scholarship that makes works such as this possible. In *Guided by a Steady Hand: The Cultural Landscape of a Rural Texas Park* (1998), Utley and Steely provided the first book-length study of a CCC-built state park in Texas, Mother Neff State Park. That book was soon followed by Steely's authoritative study *Parks for Texas: Enduring Landscapes of the New Deal* (1999). Their scholarly work and their many original contributions to The Look of Nature have been critical to chapters 1 and 2, as well as the park profiles. Fortunately, these scholars continue to contribute to our knowledge about the CCC parks. Among historians who have written more focused studies on CCC parks for TPWD are Martha Doty Freeman, Lila Knight, Terri Myers, Ralph Newlan, Julie Strong, Lonn Taylor, and Diane E. Williams. All have helped TPWD document the CCC parks for agency staff and visitors alike.

Graphics and exhibit designer Drew Patterson of Drew Patterson Studios transformed the cumulative research into a popular traveling exhibit; and interactive designer Bart Marable of Terraincognita is responsible for the handsome Look of Nature Web site. Both have enabled the CCC to reach new audiences.

Among those works on the history of the Texas State Parks Board and the TPWD, Sharon Morris Toney's "The Texas State Parks System: An Administrative History, 1923–1984" (1995) was critical, as were the reminiscences of Mike Herring and other TPWD staff and the historical timelines now in the departmental history project research files, TPWD administrative records, and other materials in the Archives and Information Services Division at the Texas State Library and Archives Commission (TSLAC).

Photo archivists Anne L. Cook at the Texas Department of Transportation (TxDOT) and John Anderson at the TSLAC have been talented and knowledgeable collaborators. Laura Saegert at the TSLAC not only catalogued the State Parks Board and TPWD collections and made our use of them much easier than it had been for previous researchers, but she also spearheaded the grant to have Texas' CCC original drawings scanned. Her efforts culminated in the Web site To Love the Beautiful (https://www.tsl.state.tx.us/exhibits/parks/), created by Liz Clare. We are grateful to those working behind the scenes at the TSLAC to care for the collections and make them available to the public: Donaly Brice, Megan Cooney, Sam Fowler, Melanie Saegert, and Sergio Velasco.

Also aiding the cause of beauty are talented photographers who enable viewers to appreciate the architecture and special scale of CCC parks: John B. Chandler, Chase Fountain, Bryan Frazier, and Earl Nottingham.

For their support, general and specific, we thank John Crain, Mike Crevier, Laura David, Nola Davis, Aina Dodge, Kevin Good, Brandon Jackobeit, Brent Leisure, Karen Leslie, Cynthia Lindlof, David Riskind, Andy Sansom, Dan Sholly, Warren Stricker, David Woodcock, and Martha Norkunas and her Interpreting-the-Texas-Past students.

For his editorial advice, generosity, and patience, we thank John Higley. Shannon Davies and Thom Lemmons are without equal as editors.

For more than five years, Angela Reed Served as archivist, oral historian, and project specialist, her skills very apparent in every role. While an agency colleague, she worked tirelessly on behalf of the CCC, most especially on the website, texascccparks.org, and this book.

Finally, we are grateful to those who have maintained, repaired, and stewarded the CCC parks over the years. We appreciate those who have supported and enjoyed the CCC parks and wish you even more trips filled with quiet walks, invigorating swims, engaging hikes, and spirited cycle rides. And for all of us who enjoy the parks, let us thank the individuals in the CCC.

ABBREVIATIONS

CCC	Civilian Conservation Corps
CWA	Civil Works Administration
DRT	Daughters of the Republic of Texas
FSA	Farm Security Administration
LCRA	Lower Colorado River Authority
NARA	National Archives and Records Administration
NPS	National Park Service
NWCG	National Wildfire Coordinating Group
NYA	National Youth Administration
PWA	Public Works Administration
TPWD	Texas Parks and Wildlife Department
TSLAC	Texas State Library and Archives Commission
TxDOT	Texas Department of Transportation
WPA	Works Progress Administration

Texas State Parks and the CCC

Tourism was an important business in Texas, and this map, drawn by NPS inspector Donald Obert and distributed by the Fort Worth Star-Telegram in 1939, shows the state's early efforts to tout its scenic features, natural resources, recreational opportunities, historic places—and CCC parks. (National Archives and Records Administration, College Park, Maryland)

The CCC Creates a Texas State Parks System

When Franklin D. Roosevelt became president in March 1933, the United States was experiencing the worst economic depression in its history. Factories had closed, banks and companies had become bankrupt, and a quarter of all workers were unemployed. Agricultural income had plummeted, and debts, exacerbated by an unprecedented drought in the Southwest, had driven many farmers from their land. To get the nation back on its feet, Roosevelt created an array of programs known collectively as the New Deal. One of these programs, the Civilian Conservation Corps (CCC), was aimed at putting young men back to work improving national and state forests and parks.

Almost 3 million Americans, most of them between the ages of eighteen and twenty-five, but including some destitute veterans of World War I and even the Spanish-American War, joined the CCC between 1933 and its disbanding not quite ten years later. An estimated fifty thousand were assigned to work in Texas during six-month enlistments, with a maximum of two years' service allowed. Guided by ideas and designs prepared by professional architects in the National Park Service (NPS), CCC enrollees constructed trails, cabins, concession buildings, bathhouses, dance pavilions, and even one hotel and a motor court to attract visitors to Texas parks.[1] Before 1930, Texas state parks had totaled just over eight hundred acres, on which fourteen state parks existed. In 1942, after CCC workers had finished transforming land into places for public recreation, there were almost sixty thousand acres and forty-eight parks.[2] By the time the companies were disbanded in 1942, CCC workers had laid the foundations for today's Texas state park system.

Understanding the Great Depression

When a typical young enrollee jumped out of a transport truck at a CCC work site in Texas, he had only limited knowledge of the circumstances that brought

A family from Oklahoma (foreground) makes their home in a California farming community's tent city for migrant workers. (FDR Library and Museum, Hyde Park, New York)

him there. He was, of course, keenly aware of his father's unemployed plight and his family's desperate need for income. He knew that jobs in his hometown were nowhere to be found and that neighboring families were in the same fix as his. But the economic forces that had brought his family and hometown to their knees were probably beyond his knowledge. To be sure, he had observed how the well-off in his town had benefited from the previous decade, the Roaring Twenties, though his family and most others he knew had gained little from that decade of financial extravagance. He knew only that whatever had happened was now being paid for many times over in the misery of relatives and friends.

The typical CCC worker, if he had reached the age of twenty-one, probably voted for the first time in 1932 and had most likely cast his ballot for Roosevelt and other Democratic Party candidates rather than Herbert Hoover and the Republicans. As president after 1928, Hoover had for four years relied mainly on reduced government spending to restore business confidence and on voluntary local and private sources of relief to lessen the average American's plight. These measures were in step with laissez-faire economic doctrines at the time. Personally, Hoover took heart from the success he had enjoyed overseeing the delivery of humanitarian aid to millions of Europeans on the brink of starvation in the wake of World War I, the Russian Revolution, and other wartime upheavals. But accepted laissez-faire ideas and largely voluntary aid efforts proved ineffective in the face of the unprecedented economic collapse that unfolded between 1930 and 1932.

Photographs taken by the Farm Security Administration (FSA) capture the hopelessness, enforced idleness, and haunted faces of millions of Americans dur-

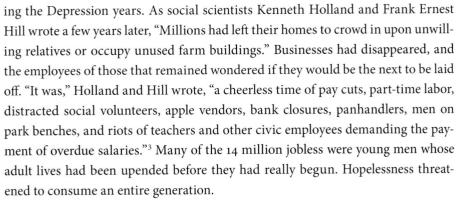

"Dust Storm Approaching Spearman, Texas, April 14, 1935." (FDR Library and Museum, Hyde Park, New York)

"Blown-Out Farm Field," ca. 1938. (National Oceanic and Atmospheric Administration/Department of Commerce, from Russell Lord, To Hold This Soil*)*

ing the Depression years. As social scientists Kenneth Holland and Frank Ernest Hill wrote a few years later, "Millions had left their homes to crowd in upon unwilling relatives or occupy unused farm buildings." Businesses had disappeared, and the employees of those that remained wondered if they would be the next to be laid off. "It was," Holland and Hill wrote, "a cheerless time of pay cuts, part-time labor, distracted social volunteers, apple vendors, bank closures, panhandlers, men on park benches, and riots of teachers and other civic employees demanding the payment of overdue salaries."[3] Many of the 14 million jobless were young men whose adult lives had been upended before they had really begun. Hopelessness threatened to consume an entire generation.

America's physical landscape was also badly degraded. For a century or more, many lands west of the Appalachians had been cleared, plowed, and grazed with abandon. Consequently, topsoil that was no longer grounded by root systems of native grasses became blowing dust as winds swept over land made dry by a disastrous drought. Six out of every ten inhabitants of the southwestern states fled to the country's West Coast to escape the terrible conditions, a migration dramatized by John Steinbeck in *The Grapes of Wrath*. Unchecked lumbering in the country's

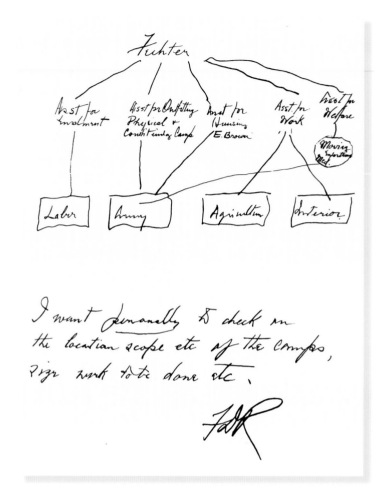

A few days prior to signing his executive order, President Roosevelt sketched on his napkin an organizational chart showing how the CCC's director Robert Fechner (whose name he misspelled) would draw upon the resources of the Departments of War, Labor, Agriculture, and the Interior. (FDR Library and Museum, Hyde Park, New York)

western regions had made lands vulnerable to floods. Where once there had been 800 million acres of forest, by 1933 only 100 million remained.

The array of New Deal programs constituted Roosevelt's response after he entered the White House. His administration quickly created federal agencies to monitor and regulate industry, employ men and women in mammoth projects like Boulder Dam, and provide others with work in community organizations funded by Washington.[4] The Works Progress Administration (WPA) alone put 8 million unemployed Americans to work on projects that ran the gamut from building roads and dams for hydroelectric power in the Tennessee Valley to writing state guidebooks and recording oral histories of former slaves.

Roosevelt sketched another idea as part of his New Deal efforts, an outline for the CCC. The hastily drawn diagram belied his long-held belief that physical vigor and spiritual health were intertwined. He knew well the precedents of European work camps to renew the spirits of soldiers and youth after the devastation of

THE CCC — A YOUNG MAN'S OPPORTUNITY

to work

to live
to learn
to build

— and to conserve our National Resources

World War I. Although only a sketch, it spoke to Roosevelt's abiding affirmation in the healing power of nature and the strengths of individuals. This was the basis of the CCC, and it proved to be a centerpiece of all these New Deal efforts.

Roosevelt proposed the CCC to Congress on March 21, 1933, just days after taking his oath of office, and the enabling legislation was quickly passed. Nicknamed sardonically "Roosevelt's Tree Army," CCC enrollees were soon rehabilitating land damaged by fires, lumbering, and erosion by planting millions of trees, digging

The flip side of this recruitment poster published from 1933 to 1942 listed applicant qualifications, living conditions, and salaries in the CCC. It also promised that the CCC could help a young man "build his self-respect, his mind, his body," so he could "make his way in the world." (Texas Parks and Wildlife Department)

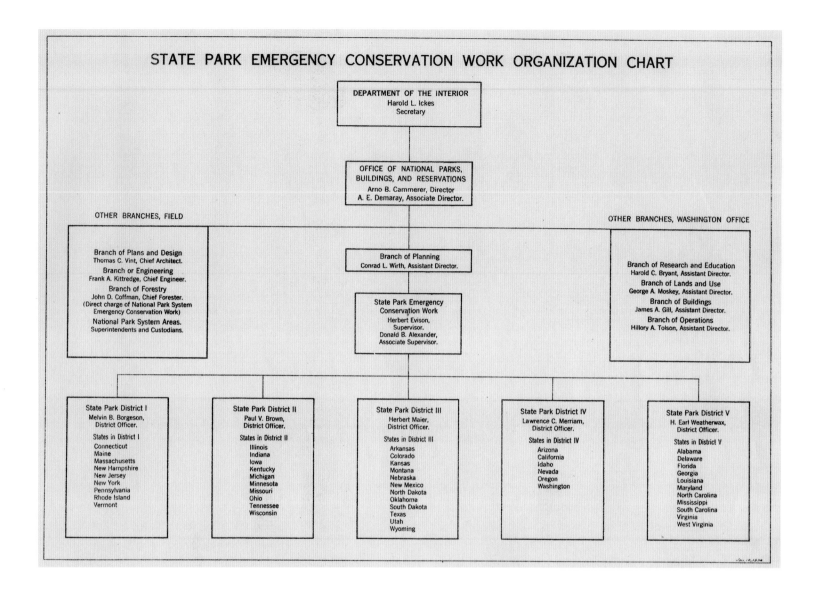

STATE PARK EMERGENCY CONSERVATION WORK ORGANIZATION CHART

DEPARTMENT OF THE INTERIOR
Harold L. Ickes
Secretary

OFFICE OF NATIONAL PARKS,
BUILDINGS, AND RESERVATIONS
Arno B. Cammerer, Director
A. E. Demaray, Associate Director.

OTHER BRANCHES, FIELD

OTHER BRANCHES, WASHINGTON OFFICE

Branch of Plans and Design
Thomas C. Vint, Chief Architect.
Branch or Engineering
Frank A. Kittredge, Chief Engineer.
Branch of Forestry
John D. Coffman, Chief Forester.
(Direct charge of National Park System
Emergency Conservation Work)
National Park System Areas.
Superintendents and Custodians.

Branch of Planning
Conrad L. Wirth, Assistant Director.

State Park Emergency
Conservation Work
Herbert Evison,
Supervisor.
Donald B. Alexander,
Associate Supervisor.

Branch of Research and Education
Harold C. Bryant, Assistant Director.
Branch of Lands and Use
George A. Moskey, Assistant Director.
Branch of Buildings
James A. Gill, Assistant Director.
Branch of Operations
Hillory A. Tolson, Assistant Director.

State Park District I	State Park District II	State Park District III	State Park District IV	State Park District V
Melvin B. Borgeson, District Officer.	Paul V. Brown, District Officer.	Herbert Maier, District Officer.	Lawrence C. Merriam, District Officer.	H. Earl Weatherwax, District Officer.
States in District I	States in District II	States in District III	States in District IV	States in District V
Connecticut	Illinois	Arkansas	Arizona	Alabama
Maine	Indiana	Colorado	California	Delaware
Massachusetts	Iowa	Kansas	Idaho	Florida
New Hampshire	Kentucky	Montana	Nevada	Georgia
New Jersey	Michigan	Nebraska	Oregon	Louisiana
New York	Minnesota	New Mexico	Washington	Maryland
Pennsylvania	Missouri	North Dakota		North Carolina
Rhode Island	Ohio	Oklahoma		Mississippi
Vermont	Tennessee	South Dakota		South Carolina
	Wisconsin	Texas		Virginia
		Utah		West Virginia
		Wyoming		

A year after Roosevelt sketched his idea for the organization of the CCC, this formal chart was in place for the Department of the Interior. The NPS had overarching duties in developing state parks. At this time, Texas fell into District III. (Administrative and subject files, Texas State Parks Board records, Texas State Library and Archives Commission)

ditches and canals, stocking lakes and rivers with upward of a billion fish, restoring historic battlefields as memorials, and building hundreds of campgrounds and structures in previously empty locations. A crucial aim of these undertakings was to revive the spirits of disheartened young men. As Roosevelt said when he introduced the CCC in an address to Congress,

> More important . . . than the material gains will be the moral and spiritual value of such work. The overwhelming majority of unemployed Americans, who are now walking the streets and receiving private or public relief, would infinitely prefer to work. We can take a vast army of these unemployed out into

healthful surroundings. We can eliminate to some extent at least the threat that enforced idleness brings to spiritual and moral stability.[5]

Despite early and strong congressional support for his CCC initiative, Roosevelt knew that public support for it was hardly universal, and some pockets of skepticism were quite vocal. Business leaders objected to the CCC's cost and a large new government bureaucracy; labor leaders worried that the CCC would undercut and lower union members' wages. Some intellectuals disposed toward socialism feared CCC camps would become breeding grounds for military regimentation akin to what rising fascist states were doing in Europe; critics fearful of socialism believed a system of CCC camps might well brainwash and radicalize workers in them.

Within a few months, nonetheless, CCC camps were dotted across the country, most of them engaged in environmental conservation, but some aimed at creating parks and other recreational facilities for public use. Initially, the Department of Labor in Washington was in charge of selecting CCC enrollees; to do this, it cooperated with county welfare agencies to find and certify enrollees. The Departments of Agriculture and the Interior selected projects for CCC camps to carry out. The War Department (today's Department of Defense) had multiple responsibilities: assess and approve CCC campsites for water supply and sanitation; supervise camp construction, maintenance, and administration; and ensure the health, welfare, and discipline of workers in the camps. The War Department was also charged with selecting and supervising camp administrative personnel, including teachers and advisers selected by the Office of Education. The Department of the Interior was responsible for planning, executing, and administering projects by hiring and supervising project directors, as well as officers to liaise between directors. Overall, the Departments of War and Interior played the most important roles: the former being responsible for camp operations; the latter, for delivering all sorts of completed projects.

Texas in the Great Depression

Texans had much to gain from Roosevelt's New Deal programs, although it took some time before many Texans comprehended just how widespread the need for these programs was in their state. Texans tended to support Hoover's mild measures to counteract the economic crisis, but being distant from "stock speculators" on Wall Street, they believed the crisis would be fleeting and Texas would be little affected. However, when economic conditions worsened steadily during 1931–1932, many Texans were forced to conclude that the government in Austin, like the government in Washington, was being overwhelmed. As a CCC enrollee who helped

In 1933, unemployed workers in San Antonio stood in line to enroll in the US Department of Labor's Employment Service, seeking assistance through the Federal Emergency Relief Administration. ("Men in Unemployment Line, San Antonio, September 1933"; L-0049-A, San Antonio Light *Photograph Collection, MS 359, University of Texas at San Antonio Libraries Special Collections from the Institute of Texan Cultures)*

These men lived in tents just outside San Antonio and waited for better luck and a revived economy. ("Itinerants in San Antonio—Hobo Jungle 1938"; L-1784-A, San Antonio Light *Photograph Collection, MS 359, University of Texas at San Antonio Libraries Special Collections from the Institute of Texan Cultures)*

build two Texas parks recalled, "I didn't know anything about the stock market, when it fell or anything like that. But I remember [in] the Depression that times were hard and nobody had anything."[6]

In the 1932 presidential campaign Roosevelt chose Representative John Nance Garner of Uvalde as his vice presidential candidate, and Texans voted resoundingly for the Democratic ticket that November. In addition to Garner, the state had many influential voices in Washington, who made sure Texas got its share of CCC and other New Deal funds. Many Texans were grateful for the chance to work in the CCC and not above resorting to a little subterfuge to get the chance. For example, upon hearing about the CCC quite by accident, one sixteen-year-old Texan was undaunted when told that enrollees had to be eighteen years of age. His informant said that the local CCC administrators might not guess his true age. "So all I needed was a suggestion," the young man later recalled. "I go in and joined. Nobody ever asked me—I told them in the beginning I was eighteen."[7] The teenager thus lowered the average age of CCC workers in Texas, which was twenty, a tiny bit.

A 1940 survey of CCC enrollees in Texas found that the men had signed up mainly to help their families.[8] Poignantly, one former enrollee remembered his sharecropper father saying to him, "'Would you mind going into the CCC for six months? It sure would help the family.' I said, 'Dad, I will do anything to help our family.'"[9] This enrollee and many like him did more than help their families; through laborious work they built a park system for Texas.

Texas Parks before the CCC

During the 1920s, a few prominent Texans argued strongly for creating state parks. One in particular was especially influential and vocal: Pat Neff, who as governor from 1921 until 1925 was the chief proponent of a state park system. One of Neff's predecessors in the Governor's Mansion, Thomas Campbell, had earlier listened to "the ladies" in the Daughters of the Republic of Texas (DRT), an organization that had lobbied long and hard to acquire and preserve historic Texas landmarks, most especially the Alamo. In 1907, Governor Campbell designated San Jacinto Battleground as a state park. Campbell's successor, Governor Oscar Colquitt, then designated Gonzales State Park; and *his* successor, James Ferguson, designated Washington-on-the-Brazos to commemorate the place where Texas independence was declared in 1836.[10]

Historical parks commemorating past events were part of a national "colonial revival" movement oriented to the pre–Civil War era. By about 1910, Texas was eager to mark its 1836 triumph in the revolution against Mexican rule and turn

The Political Web to Washington

Texas connections with Washington were strong in the 1930s. Paramount among them was John Nance Garner of Uvalde, former speaker of the house and now vice president, for whom Garner State Park was later named. Keenly aware of Garner's strong political connections in Washington, President Roosevelt needed Garner's influence to pass his programs by securing southern Democratic votes in Congress. He got what he needed with the help of the powerful Texan.

Representative Sam Rayburn, later speaker of the house, was also a proponent of the CCC, as was Congressman Richard M. Kleburg, the namesake of CCC "Camp Kleberg" [*sic*] at Lake Corpus Christi. As a secretary to Representative Kleburg, Lyndon B. Johnson, his presidency still decades ahead, was new to the Washington scene. His contacts nevertheless led to appointment as head of Roosevelt's National Youth Administration (NYA), another New Deal program.

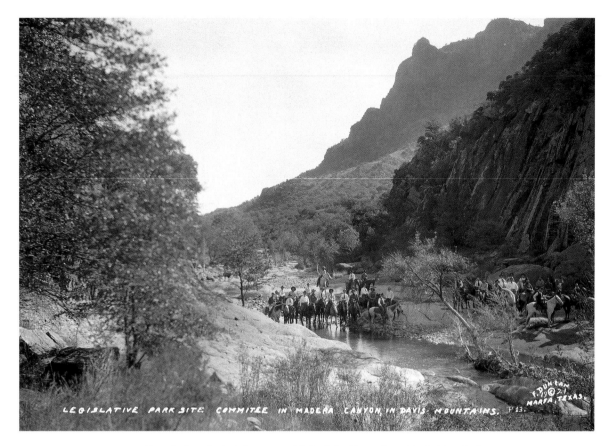

LEGISLATIVE PARK SITE COMMITEE IN MADERA CANYON, IN DAVIS MOUNTAINS. P 13.

Even before the legislature established the Texas State Parks Board, there was interest in having state parks. Here, the Legislative Park Site Committee explores the Davis Mountains. Within fifteen years, Indian Lodge, Davis Mountains, and Balmorhea State Parks, as well as Big Bend National Park (at first a state park), were constructed by the CCC. (Duncan Photographic Collection, Marfa and Presidio County Museum Association)

away from Civil War defeat.[11] The colonial revival movement meshed with a burgeoning regard for nature, broadly construed. Reflecting this, the NPS was created in 1916, and its first director, the inspirational Stephen Mather, convened a National Conference on State Parks in 1921 to encourage state and local systems of parks that would complement a national parks system.

In step with or even ahead of his contemporaries, soon after becoming governor in January 1921, Pat Neff devised a plan for a system of parks that went beyond historical monuments and parks to showcase the diversity of Texas' landscape, encourage tourism, and promote conservation.[12] In 1923, Neff persuaded the state legislature to approve the framework for a park system, although the legislature then declined, repeatedly, to appropriate funds for purchasing parklands or mak-

Taken in San Antonio in July 1924, this photo of the Texas State Parks Board may have been on the occasion of planning one of several caravans through rural Texas to solicit donations from landowners for roadside parks. From left to right, David E. Colp of San Antonio, chairman; Phebe K. Warner of Claude, secretary and statistician; Pat M. Neff of Waco, governor; Mrs. W. C. Martin of Dallas, vice chairman; Robert M. Hubbard of Texarkana, chairman of State Highway Commission; Katie Welder of Victoria, historian; and Hobart Key of Marshall, attorney and sergeant at arms. (Civilian Conservation Corps files, State Parks Board records, TSLAC)

Roadside parks ranged from sites with a few amenities to those with only a small parcel of land. This roadside park in Williamson County on US Highway 81 offered a chance to cook out, picnic, and camp. (Texas Department of Transportation)

ing improvements to lands already donated to the state. In 1925, and despite Neff's staunch advocacy, a state parks bill stalled in the legislature and lay there until Margie Elizabeth Neal, the first woman senator in Texas, resurrected it two years later.[13]

Miriam "Ma" Ferguson, Texas' first woman governor, nudged the fledgling park system forward early in her second (nonconsecutive) term of office, which

"Texas Governor Miriam Ferguson Signing a Bill, Austin, c. 1933." With former governor Pat Neff seated to Governor Ferguson's left, the occasion for this photograph was likely Ferguson's formal announcement that the state, for the first time, had given the State Parks Board a budget line, an action essential for securing federal funds. (Photo courtesy of the Bell County Museum, Belton, Texas)

Summarizing the tasks of the State Park Emergency Conservation Work, young men planted trees and built parks according to designs presented by the superintendent. Besides depicting the company's camp and the attractive bridge, waterfall, and stairs, this illustration communicated the "emergency" nature of the work as the men hastened to roof the refectory while eager Americans rushed to take advantage of new facilities. (TSLAC)

began in 1933. Within days of Roosevelt's announcement of his CCC initiative, Ferguson sought and obtained federal funds for twenty-six CCC projects in Texas, including the construction of fifteen state parks.[14] She directed her newly created Texas Relief Commission to help recruit and place workers at these park projects, a task she assigned to the State Parks Board later in 1933. Previously, the state government had relied on convict labor to maintain parks supervised by the Parks Board, but by the end of 1933 companies of CCC enrollees had arrived at locations for new parks to be built without convict workers.

Federal funds poured into Texas for soil projects and park development during 1933, the Great Depression's worst year.[15] Ferguson's successor, James Allred, further reduced unemployment in the state by obtaining funds for additional CCC projects and for other projects funded by the NYA, the WPA, and the Public Works Administration (PWA).[16] But it was with the CCC's arrival that a proper state park system began to take form.

Designing CCC Parks

Master plans drawn up for the new parks by veteran NPS architects specified improved roads that would bring automobile visitors through formal portals made of local stone, followed by drives on roads with modern "super-elevated" curves that crossed carefully crafted stone bridges and culverts.[17] According to the plans, visitors would typically arrive at a refectory or concession building, also made of local stone and wood, where they would be able to obtain park information, use areas for groups to gather, purchase food and supplies for camping, take advantage of well-constructed restrooms, and have patios available for outdoor dancing and other activities. Master plans for parks with lakes specified boathouses and beach shelters, and for parks with swimming pools, bathhouses and play areas. Plans for larger parks, such as those to be built at Bastrop, Lake Brownwood, Daingerfield, Garner, and Palo Duro Canyon, provided designs for simple cabins to be used for overnight and longer stays. Service facilities at the parks were to have distinctively rustic water towers, keepers' lodges, and maintenance areas tucked away from the key public buildings.

To get the CCC park projects started, the Department of the Interior asked the NPS to specify what building methods CCC workers would use and how park landscapes should look. Having designed and built national parks such as Yellowstone, Glacier, and Grand Canyon previously, the NPS employed models used for those parks to plan state parks. In Texas and other states, the NPS required the State Parks Board or its equivalent to set up on-site offices with drafting tables, maps of park boundaries, areas within the boundaries that were to be altered or left

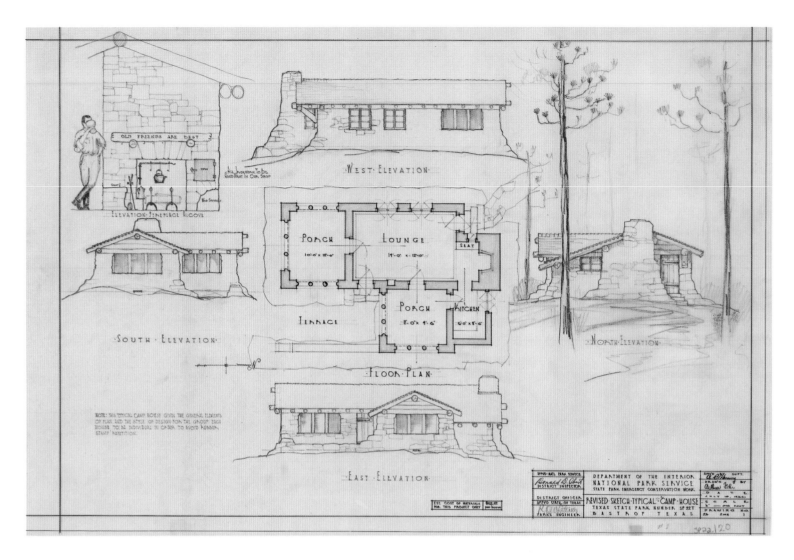

Completed by architect Arthur Fehr on July 10, 1934, these revised sketches of a typical camp house provided the basic elements used in varied arrangements to individualize each planned cabin for Bastrop State Park. (TSLAC)

untouched, and indications of how people and automobiles were expected to circulate in the parks.

Herbert Maier, the NPS acting director in charge of park projects in Texas, was an accomplished architect who had designed park structures for Yellowstone, Yosemite, and Glacier National Parks during the 1920s. Maier was instrumental in laying down design standards to govern the work of architects, planners, and inspectors in Texas. NPS Assistant Director Conrad Wirth and Herb Evison, who was in charge of NPS cooperation with state parks, together with George Nason, the senior NPS inspector for Texas, did much to translate Maier's architectural visions into reality.

These men, especially Maier, were influenced by prevailing notions of nature's beauty that had evolved over several decades and become a credo for park archi-

A board-and-batten office of the NPS, Department of the Interior, stood on the grounds of Lake Corpus Christi State Park during its construction. Outlined with small stones, "SP-32-T" signifies that it was a state park project, Park 32, Texas. (TPWD)

In 1936, NPS officials visited the Big Bend in Texas and Mexico. Architect Herbert Maier, the leading architect for park designs nationwide and in Texas, is seated on the ground as he and a team of inspectors pause for a photograph while touring the region. (NARA, College Park, Maryland)

Herbert Maier designed Yellowstone National Park's Madison Museum (photographed in 1929). It was considered one of the best examples of rustic architecture in the NPS and served as a model for Texas park buildings during the 1930s. (Library of Congress Prints and Photographs Division)

tects and planners. Both Frederick Law Olmsted's naturalistic parks and Henry Hobson Richardson's use of materials in his heavy stone buildings anticipated new structures blending seamlessly with their natural settings. The parks and buildings of Olmsted, Richardson, and their contemporaries greatly influenced the arts and crafts movement, which during the twentieth-century's early years sought alternatives to revivalist historical styles and factory-like buildings that had stemmed from the Industrial Revolution. Publications such as *The Craftsman* spread new architectural ideals to a wide audience, making rustic stone bungalows and handmade

NPS state park inspector George L. Nason held degrees in landscape architecture and engineering, ideal qualifications for advising the younger architects and CCC workers who assembled buildings and shaped landscapes. (Courtesy of the George Nason family)

Herbert Evison (left), NPS state park coordinator, and Conrad Wirth, NPS assistant director, personally inspected CCC projects in Texas during 1935. They are pictured here in the Big Bend. (National Park Service, Harpers Ferry Center)

furnishings popular. The iconoclastic Frank Lloyd Wright also disdained formal architectural styles and developed an "organic architecture" in which buildings "grew" naturally from their environments and took forms that reflected qualities of the materials used to construct them. NPS architects gave life to these newly fashionable ideas in parks they designed during the 1920s and 1930s.

Although used primarily for the design of suburban houses and other types of buildings, the ideas of Olmsted, Richardson, Wright, and others were well suited to parks in natural settings. Previously, resort hotels in remote areas embodied the ornate style of Victorian architecture, with elaborate wood exteriors painted and trimmed in vermilion or Paris green from top to bottom. Finding these artifacts of the Victorian era jarring to the eye when located in a dense forest, near a hot spring, on a canyon rim, or nestled at the base of a majestic mountain, designers during the 1920s and 1930s strove for styles more in tune with such landscapes. The plans they provided for CCC parks were for structures that would be unobtrusive in natural settings. They were to consist of local stone, timber, and other materials easily obtainable in or near where each park would be located. The construction of buildings would involve straightforward masonry and carpentry techniques, and buildings would have simple horizontal lines and low silhouettes that would not distract from the natural setting each park celebrated.

Frank Lloyd Wright designed the Frederick C. Robie House (1908) in the Prairie style that Wright made popular. It featured low horizontal roof lines parallel with the ground, which contrasted with the height of surrounding trees. Tyler, Bonham, and Daingerfield State Parks, all constructed by the CCC, were designed with Wright's principles in mind. (Library of Congress Prints and Photographs Division)

The bathhouse at Tyler State Park was designed in the Prairie style popularized by Frank Lloyd Wright. (Photo by John B. Chandler, 2008, TPWD)

The Roots of Park Design

Nineteenth-century American park planner Frederick Law Olmsted believed that park landscapes should invite the visitor to feel closer to nature, engage the senses, and elicit an emotional response to one's surroundings. In his "Notes on the Plan of Franklin Park," Olmsted wrote that roads, for example, should "provide for a constant mild enjoyment of simply pleasing rural scenery while in easy movement." One of Olmsted's contemporaries, Andrew Jackson Downing, prescribed park trails that should lead a visitor pleasantly from one natural experience to another.

Drawing inspiration from Olmsted and Downing, the NPS designed and the CCC built trails leading from pavilions nestled in woodlands to shelters overlooking scenic vistas. Buildings along with picnic tables, fire pits, and benches—what Downing called "embellishments" in his book *The Theory and Practice of Landscape Gardening*—were purposefully placed within nature. The shapes, materials, and locations continue to appeal to visitors, inviting them to relax within landscapes and experience solitude yet feel protected from "the wild."

The refectory roof at Palmetto State Park was originally constructed with palmetto fronds to make use of local materials and blend with the environment. However, maintenance concerns won out and wooden shakes now form its roof. (TPWD)

Local limestone was used to construct the pavilion at Blanco State Park. (John B. Chandler, 2011, TPWD)

Shellcrete blocks were constructed on-site at both Goose Island and Lake Corpus Christi State Parks. (NARA, College Park, Maryland)

These designs and construction techniques produced many structures pleasing to the eye in Texas. Vibrant red sandstone formed the Romanesque arches of the signature concession building at Abilene State Park. Locally harvested timber was used in Lockhart and Bastrop State Parks, with roof shingles cut from its lengths. Thatches of palmetto leaves were used for the roof of the remarkable refectory at Palmetto State Park. Locally quarried limestone, plentiful in some areas of Texas, formed building walls and other features at Longhorn Cavern and Blanco State Parks. To avoid buildings being humdrum, designers specified imaginative combinations of local materials, for example, stone and wood at Bastrop State Park, but stone and adobe at Davis Mountains State Park. Directed by NPS planners, CCC enrollees even developed the idea to create a concrete mix consisting of cement and locally available sand and oyster shell at Goose Island and Lake Corpus Christi State Parks.

Everywhere, NPS architects, regionally based and working with Parks Board architects stationed in Austin and at the various parks, endeavored to create a cultural landscape infused with the philosophy of naturalism. They regarded every building, picnic shelter, and signpost as a potentially intrusive element—an "infection," as one CCC manual put it—to be harmonized to the maximum extent possible with the environment surrounding it.

The strong emphasis on low horizontal rather than sharply vertical buildings and other structures stemmed from what Herbert Maier termed "the Horizontal Key." As architectural historian James Wright Steely describes this, "You see a consistent horizontal orientation of the fabric—no matter what the fabric is. And that puts it in line with the ground, close to the ground."[18] Employing arches as a central

From this angle, the Bastrop cabin appears to "hug" the earth as the red sandstone splays at the bottom. From the highest elevation, the roofline appears to touch the ground and the cabin to be tucked into the hillside. (TPWD)

Arches were designed for the combination building to create a Spanish-style colonnade at Garner State Park. (John B. Chandler, 2008, TPWD)

design element helped implement Maier's Horizontal Key. In Texas and elsewhere, NPS architects routinely insisted on arches that would break up the facades of park buildings and blend them with the landscape. Visually, arches provide an orderly rhythm in large structures, and they figure prominently in many imposing buildings the CCC built in Texas.

Locations of buildings and other structures were also governed by the credo of unobtrusiveness. Designers and planners worked hard to select locations where structures would appear as simple extensions of the ground on which they sat. For example, the cabins and shelters at Bastrop State Park seem part of a natural

At Palo Duro Canyon State Park the stone facade of the interpretive center, originally known as the Coronado Lodge, was designed to mimic the canyon wall. For this photo, art students in a class from West Texas State University in Canyon, Texas, perched on the canyon rim for a lesson in sketching scenery in 1944. (Panhandle-Plains Historical Museum, Canyon, Texas)

depression in the ground. The Palo Duro Canyon State Park interpretive center, originally designed as a lodge by NPS architect Guy Carlander, perches on the canyon's rim and seems an extension of the cliff wall below it. Whether located at high or low elevations, park structures were always subordinated to the landscape and often made it more interesting.

Ingenious visual and tactile blending extended to screening some park infrastructures. Designers kept complex and necessarily "unnatural" mechanical and maintenance systems generally out of public view, and where at all possible they designed them according to the NPS aesthetic. To minimize intrusiveness, roadway designs sought to limit speed and noise and allow automobiles to glide through natural settings. Below and to the sides of park roads, stone-lined drainages and culverts were in harmony with the stone construction of bridges. Walking trails meandered to scenic overlooks with stone benches for viewing pleasure. At well-situated picnic areas, stone ovens and tables were inviting to hungry visitors.

In the park designs, maintaining continuity with the past was as important as achieving continuity with landscapes. The NPS philosophy of architecture held that park structures should reflect the history and material culture of the local region. So, in heavily forested Northeast Texas where log houses and stores had dotted the landscape during the nineteenth and early twentieth centuries,

L. C. Fuller took this photo on May 21, 1936, at Bonham State Park. As attractive and sturdy as the oven is, the park official was pleased that it was out of view: "A substancial [sic] incinerator located inside the service yard at rear of combination bldg. Completely hidden from view from all locations except inside the service yard." (TPWD)

Believed to be design staff with the State Parks Board, two men pose on a pine footbridge in Bastrop State Park. Laced throughout the park are stone-lined culverts designed to channel flowing creeks. (TPWD)

This picnic table at Blanco State Park stretches some seventy feet in length. Its concrete top rests on waist-high masonry pedestals. The bench seats that completely surround the table are constructed of stone, as is the nearby fireplace. (TPWD)

Designers called for log veneer at Caddo Lake State Park buildings not only to point to the natural materials abundant in the Texas Piney Woods but also to fit in with the vernacular architecture of the region. (John B. Chandler, 2001, TPWD)

Photographed in 1935 just after completion, Indian Lodge was constructed of indigenous clay formed into adobe bricks and blended almost seamlessly into the landscape. (Archives of the Big Bend)

Built with stone from the site and a nearby quarry, Mission Nuestra Señora del Espíritu Santo de Zúñiga at Goliad State Park and Historic Site was a reconstruction intended to remind visitors of Texas' Spanish past. (Stan A. Williams, 2010, TxDOT)

architects prescribed log structures for Caddo Lake State Park. They even directed CCC workers at Caddo to use half-log veneers for the exterior walls of their barracks so the barracks could later be converted into cabins for park visitors without departing from the log motif. The design for Indian Lodge in Davis Mountains State Park drew inspiration from Native American pueblos in nearby New Mexico. At Goliad, and at the behest of local citizens, notably County Judge James Arthur White, NPS preservation architects and archeologists improved the state historical park, originally created in 1907, by guiding CCC workers in the reconstruction of several buildings from the extensive ruins of the eighteenth-century

In 1935, Judge White and planners of the Texas Centennial secured a CCC company that consisted of older war veterans to restore mission buildings and install campgrounds along the curving San Antonio River. This beautiful drawing served as the cover sheet for that Goliad Master Plan and was likely drawn by Samuel Vosper, D. D. Obert, Raiford Stripling, and T. Phinney. Their artistic drawings for the extensive Goliad CCC work form a colorful, enduring, and invaluable collection. (TSLAC)

Spanish Mission Nuestra Señora del Espíritu Santo de Zúñiga. Architect Samuel C. P. Vosper and his understudies Raiford L. Stripling and Chester Nagel researched missions in Mexico similar to the mission that had existed at Goliad to guide its reconstruction.

These designs and plans for a score of new or upgraded state parks set the stage for construction work by some of the fifty thousand CCC enrollees in Texas during the next ten years. The experiences and lives of these generally young CCCers are the subject of the next chapter.

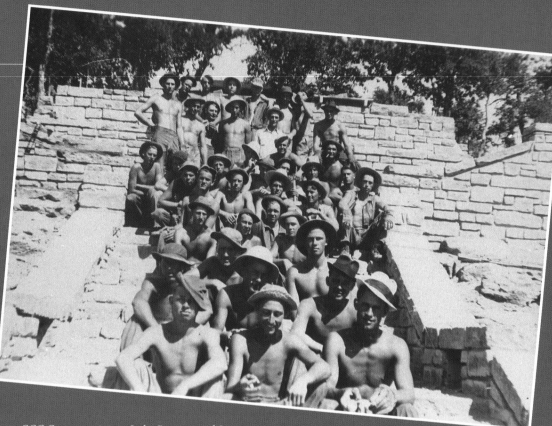

CCC Company 849 at Lake Brownwood State
Park poses for a photograph with their impressive construction feat
as backdrop. Enrollees learned, probably from the shirted supervisor in their midst, how to build
the lookout shelter atop the elegant stairway that leads to the pier on the lake. (NARA, College
Park, Maryland)

Building CCC Parks in Texas

After the first CCC camp in the United States opened in Virginia in April 1933, Texas was quick to follow suit, and its first CCC camp opened a month later in Kirbyville. The nearly fifty thousand people who worked in the CCC in Texas during the next decade were organized in some two hundred companies and provided the state with millions of dollars' worth of labor.[1] The CCC's contributions to Texas included reforestation, erosion control, and soil conservation, in addition to parks, cabins, and other recreational facilities that helped boost tourism. The CCC broadened young men's cultural and geographical horizons, including those Texan enrollees sent to work at camps located in other states. For many of those young men, it was the first time in their lives they had a regular job, earned a steady but modest paycheck, and ate three square meals a day.

Land and Men for CCC Camps

The Texas lands for which park designs were created varied greatly across the state. When the federal government solicited proposals, Governor Ferguson rushed a list of ready-made projects, including parks, to Washington. No doubt some included recommendations by Lawrence Westbrook and his Texas Relief Commission, the agency charged initially with enlisting applicants for the new CCC. The commission even began acquiring land donations for parks until the State Parks Board, led by Chairman D. E. Colp, flexed its muscles and declared its intention to take responsibility for all park work in Texas. Having evaluated lands for parks during the 1920s, the board already had its eye on certain areas, such as the Davis Mountains and Caddo Lake.

With new district offices established nationwide, the NPS was poised to process and review applications for projects, notably parks, and then plan and supervise CCC work on them. In Texas and other states, communities were invited to

Trees and Lillies in Jealous Competion in
Beautiful Caddo Lake, Caddo State Park

The Mourning Cypress Mirrored in Historical
Caddo Lake, Caddo State Park

Long recognized as a beautiful place, Caddo Lake was photographed and labeled by a poetic district engineer in East Texas for the area's photo album and sent to Texas Department of Transportation headquarters in Austin. (TxDOT)

solicit a CCC project and funds. To do this, however, a community was required to designate a minimum of five hundred acres it was willing to donate to the state and to then convince state and national CCC officials that the land would make an excellent park location.

Wanting to bolster their bids, some Texas communities, acting in concert with the Parks Board and NPS, designated land in or around a unique feature, such as the Lost Pines at Bastrop, the Rutledge Bog at Palmetto, or San Solomon Springs at Balmorhea. But other communities identified submarginal farmlands they could easily dispense with and for which they would happily welcome new uses. Still others designated lands adjacent to historic sites, probably realizing that the CCC

San Solomon Spring - Toyahvale
Irrigates about 11,000 acres of
Alfalfa, Oats, Vegetables, etc.

THEN --

-- AND --

-- NOW

The Largest Outdoor Swimming Pool in the World

From the district engineer in far West Texas, this photo album page features the CCC accomplishments at San Solomon Springs. What had been a cienega *was harnessed to become the "largest outdoor swimming pool in the world." (TxDOT)*

projects they sought would coincide with the approach of the Texas Centennial celebrations in 1936, thus heightening chances that the parks they proposed would be selected. This was probably the case, for example, when Albany proposed Fort Griffin and Mexia designated land proximate to Old Fort Parker near what became Fort Parker State Park.

Distinctive geographic features such as the Davis Mountains and coastal areas like Goose Island provided obvious settings for parks, as did tourist magnets like Palo Duro Canyon and Longhorn Cavern.[2] Not surprisingly, the selection process often favored influential Texas politicians such as Sam Rayburn of Bonham and John Nance Garner of Uvalde.[3] Lyndon Baines Johnson ensured his Hill Country

New recruits were eager to register for work wherever the CCC would have them. These young men from Clinton, Oklahoma, are in Philadelphia in transit to their worksite. (NARA, College Park, Maryland)

would have several parks and that some CCC camps in Texas were renewed for successive six-month periods. Meanwhile, the NPS and Parks Board heard the voices of local and regional politicians who, along with motivated citizens, helped swing decisions in favor of projects.

It was the task of CCC enrollees to implement NPS-approved master plans, developed by architects who worked for the State Parks Board and who were funded by the NPS. With youth on their side and relatively elastic time frames for completing park construction, CCC workers chipped rocks out of quarries and hauled wood for park buildings. Most of this work required limited technical training; the premium was on hard manual labor under a usually blazing sun. "Locally experienced men" (LEMs) were hired to supervise this manual labor. The LEMs were mature artisans with carpentry, stone masonry, electrical, plumbing, or blacksmithing skills that enabled them to guide teams of unskilled workers.

Some CCC enrollees hailed from nearby Texas farming communities, but many came from distant cities in the northeastern United States and had been rounded up to get them off the streets. Few had more than an elementary education, and most had little job experience or training beyond simple farm duties or other rudimentary work. Having subsisted on meager diets lacking much nutrition, enrollees tended to be underweight, some quite severely. All arrived at camps in which workmates and bosses were strangers.

Upon their arrival, enrollees received vaccinations and a modest package of items for personal hygiene. They were also issued a uniform, usually an ill-fitting

CCC camps, typically highly structured and organized, were laid out like military bases. At Palmetto State Park the mess hall, kitchen, and recreation hall were centrally located and flanked by the barracks arranged in a grid pattern. (NARA, College Park, Maryland)

Physical training was a requirement for enrollees before breakfast and the workday began. (NARA, College Park, Maryland)

Enrollees at Balmorhea State Park enjoy a library of books, magazines, and newspapers. (NARA, College Park, Maryland)

one. As a former enrollee named Otto Pruetz recalled, "Well, I guess you could call it a uniform. They were all blue jeans. I think they were all one size." Holding his arms out wide, Pruetz laughed and said, "They were all about this big around. They gave us several of those jeans and jackets, too, like blue jean jackets. We trimmed them all up, though. We cut the sleeves off the jackets."[4]

Encountering fellow enrollees for the first time, each young man tried to settle into a barracks devoid of personal comforts, knowing only that he would at least receive three meals a day, a cash stipend for his five-day workweek, lodging, clothes, and footwear, as well as medical and dental care. But he did not know how his days would be filled.

When reveille sounded in the morning at 6:00 a.m., the new camp inhabitant found out what was in store.[5] He was required to make his bed, help clean the barracks, and participate in a morning exercise routine led by one of his company's officers before sitting down to a breakfast of eggs, bacon, cereal, and milk. He then drew the day's tools and reported to a job site. After a morning of hard work, he ate lunch back at camp or munched a sandwich at the job site before resuming work until late in the afternoon. Returning to camp, he enjoyed an evening consisting of supper and some combination of a study program, library time, and recreation that often involved a competitive team sport before it was time for lights out. US Army personnel controlled the living arrangements in CCC camps, and enrollees were subjected to a military regimen in the camp. However, work sites were supervised by representatives of one or another federal agency, usually the NPS, Forest Service, or Soil Conservation Service.

Work in the Camps

Although camp life was quasi-military in form, CCC enrollees performed civilian work outlined in the master plan, typically directed by supervisors and LEMs charged with getting approved projects completed within each six-month period. Armed with the master plan, camp superintendents assigned the tasks: building a road, erecting a water tower, constructing cabins, or cutting and laying out trails. In conjunction with NPS-funded State Parks Board architects, planners, and inspectors, the superintendents were required to provide an estimate of the man-days, equipment, materials, and funds needed for each park project. They filled out a standard Job Application and Completion Record form that required justifying the project in question before sending it to the regional office of the NPS and then Washington for final approval.

Almost invariably, park construction took longer than initially anticipated. Estimates often had an easier-said-than-done character, with many changes and

The first and most extensive CCC project at Palo Duro Canyon State Park in 1933 was building a two-lane automobile road from the rim headquarters area to the floor of the canyon. Although the enrollees used dynamite and had dump trucks at their disposal, they accomplished much of the work by hand. (NARA, College Park, Maryland)

During construction of Buescher State Park, an inspector tours the red sandstone pump house with its central water tower and flanking wings that would eventually house the machinery. (TPWD)

refinements necessary as construction progressed. Park projects came close to stalling for various reasons. Some superintendents deliberately lowballed estimates of the time, equipment, and funds needed in order to prolong their camp's existence or conceal what architects really had in mind for a park. Illnesses among workers, heavy rains, extreme heat, supply shortages, equipment failures, and other unforeseen problems caused delays superintendents had to explain. There was a tendency as well to overestimate the abilities of CCC workers. As Garner State Park Acting Superintendent Ewart G. Carney wrote sardonically when seeking to justify a

Atop Scenic Mountain, the caretaker's residence at Big Spring State Park was taking shape. With the lower courses of stonework in place on the south facade of the building, the members of this work group shape walls and set window frames in place. (TPWD)

Having recently completed a concrete picnic table, workers at Goose Island State Park consult plans for directions on how to construct the benches that will line up to the reinforcing steel. (TPWD)

Each park needed an office where camp officers, NPS designers, and the Parks Board could meet, plan, and keep records. (unidentified Texas park, TPWD)

UNITED STATES
DEPARTMENT OF THE INTERIOR
NATIONAL PARK SERVICE
EMERGENCY ACTIVITIES

Tex.
Symbol No. SP-43-T.

JOB APPLICATION AND COMPLETION RECORD

Region **111** State **Texas.** Area **Goliad State Park.**

Name of job **Rest. Histroic Structure, Church** Form 7 No. **1016** Job No. **103**

Location of job **Mission Espiritu Santo** Master plan No. **Gol.-9100-6** Working plan No. **9111-7** Gol.-

BLOCK A—PROPOSED WORK

Months NUMBER OF PERIODS REQUIRED TO COMPLETE JOB (4)	WORK CONTEMPLATED			ESTIMATED COSTS			TOTAL
	UNIT	NUMBER UNITS	MAN-DAYS MAN-HOURS	LABOR	MATERIALS	EQUIPMENT	
Previously approved	No.	1	34871	$502.50	$8929.97		$9432.47
Original or additional request	No		4663		848.56		848.56
TOTAL	x x x x		39534	502.50	9778.53		10281.03

BLOCK B—LABOR SUMMARY

TYPE OF LABOR	UNSKILLED	INTERMEDIATE	SKILLED	PROFESSIONAL AND TECHNICAL	TOTAL
Number of man-hours					
Cost of labor					

Submitted by _Raiford F. Stripling_ Title **Supt. SP-43-T** Date **1/20/39**

BLOCK C—CLEARANCE

PARK AUTHORITY	DATE	PROCUREMENT OFFICER	DATE	INSPECTOR	DATE
JanWhite	1/20/39.				

BLOCK D—COMPLETION RECORD

WORK ACCOMPLISHED			TOTAL ENCUMBRANCES COMPLETED JOB				
DATE OF COMPLETION	UNIT	NUMBER UNITS	MAN-DAYS MAN-HOURS	LABOR	MATERIALS	EQUIPMENT	TOTAL	BALANCE

_____ ed by _W.F. Ayres_ Title **INSPECTOR** Date _____ Release date **JAN 21 1939**

Raiford Stripling, the historical architect who directed the reconstruction of Mission Nuestra Señora del Espíritu Santo de Zúñiga at Goliad State Park, documented his request for additional "man days" and materials in this official NPS form in 1939. In a subsequent letter he explained that the extra time and cost were due to the high level of skill required to create ornamental, molded stonework and to the unusual and necessary thickness of the walls that required additional plaster. (NARA, Denver)

project's extension, "Additional man days justified because of our necessary use of *green* cypress timber and *green* enrollee carpenter crews."[6]

Camp commanders, superintendents, and landscape and construction foremen took their jobs seriously. They tried to absorb and implement instructions contained in CCC manuals provided specifically for them. These manuals, such as one titled *CCC Foremanship*, discussed supervisory roles as well as methods for teaching safety and skills to enrollees. The manuals urged company officers to recognize that circumstances prompting enrollments were often not of enrollees' own making and to exercise patience and tact when dealing with their charges. A central theme was how to motivate young men.

Enrollees at Tyler State Park receive instructions from a LEM, ca. 1938. (NARA, College Park, Maryland)

The LEM at the left of this photo is supervising workers as they build the low-water crossing at Palmetto State Park on April 9, 1935. (TPWD)

The manuals for work supervisors covered other things to be taught, such as *Landscape Conservation*, *Construction of Trails*, *Brick and Stone Work*, and *Carpentry Joints and Splices*. Knowledge of the manuals was essential for laying out work tasks and getting them completed efficiently. An enrollee named Joe James, who worked in camps at both the Palmetto and Lake Corpus Christi State Parks, recalled an assistant leader who knew how to get things done by organizing workers' tasks. That leader carefully marked long pieces of stone with a pencil to show his men where to break stones. But at the same time, James remembered, "He had other guys waiting to put the mortar in. Some guys were mixing mortar. Some

A panoramic photograph of construction at Lake Corpus Christi State Park illustrates the coordination required for large-scale masonry projects. (TPWD)

were cutting rocks. . . . There were different sized rocks . . . little ones and big ones and cut cattycorner rocks and all that sort of thing."[7]

There was plenty of need to break rocks, especially for dam and road construction, and even the most unskilled enrollees could do that. Enrollee Russell Cashion recalled that his first job in the camp at Cleburne was breaking rocks with a sledgehammer as part of a road-building crew. Because there were few or no power drills, large rocks had to be dynamited and then broken into manageable pieces with sledgehammers.[8] In the words of Lolo Baeza, an enrollee who helped build three parks in far West Texas, "Picks and shovels. Picks and shovels. They didn't have all these big machines then."[9]

Edward Dutchover, who worked with Lolo Baeza building Indian Lodge in the Davis Mountains, remembered all the rock work needed to shape a natural spring into a swimming pool at nearby Balmorhea: "We used to go out to the mountains. We had a rock quarry. We used to go there and get rocks. Then we'd bring them to the camp and chisel them over there, face rocks and top rocks and everything. Then the guys lay them. It took a long time to build that swimming pool. A lot of rock making. You've seen Balmorhea; it's nice."[10]

Gardner Hill worked at Lake Brownwood and remembered sandstone "just under the surface of the ground. . . . If you just want to dig down—we'd dig down a little bit and then work it up, work it to the top." After a good long while during which "what I did mostly was get the rock out of the ground," Hill's skill increased so that "I finally got to the point where I could help them cut it. You know, square it up, make building blocks out of it. . . . With a small chipping hammer—is what we called it—and we'd scrub a line on that sandstone and you could chip it off and make a pretty face on it . . . an exterior face on it."[11]

Some enrollees were fortunate in avoiding the backbreaking work of extracting, cutting, and chipping stones. Located in the camp at Garner, James Garner recalled sculpting wood taken from cypress trees on the banks of the Frio and

Enrollees build strength as they break rocks in advance of constructing the dam at Cleburne State Park. (TPWD)

Building roads like this one at Palmetto State Park consisted of manpower rather than engine power. Enrollees had only pickaxes, shovels, and wheelbarrows to move soil and rocks. (TPWD)

Sabinal Rivers. Like him, other enrollees remembered with pride the carpentry work they did for park buildings and structures. They cut cedar for footbridges, trimmed lumber for building frames, carved wood for furniture, and made roof shingles: "For the shakes on the roof, they cut a block of wood, and they had it set up so that it went through the saw at an angle. It started out at about an inch, or whatever the thickness on the bottom of that shingle is, and it tapered out to just about nothing on the edge. They run that block through once, then flipped it over and run it through again to keep the grain straight. They manufactured all those shingles here."[12] Elsewhere, adobe bricks were fashioned, as Lolo Baeza remembered about Indian Lodge: "We had a frame thing that made two adobes at a time.

During the final stages of pool construction at Balmorhea State Park, Company 1856 prepared and fitted together stone sections in the wading area after the walls had been finished. The individuals at topside tables are rough-working the stone, and those in the pool bottom are fitting the stones. Pool construction alone used about thirty thousand square feet of hand-finished stone. (TPWD)

CCC workers were well along in the construction process of the refectory at Bastrop State Park when this photo was taken ca. 1936. Much of the masonry work was in place, but enrollees still needed to work the stone and frame the roof. (NARA, College Park, Maryland)

Those times, we mix it in a wheelbarrow. Mix a little grass to the mud. . . . Then put it in the thing there with a shovel. Smooth it out with your hand or a float, something like that. Then wait about five minutes and lift it up and put another."[13]

Camps at some park sites had well-known "specialty shops." The blacksmith shop in the Garner camp was famously productive, and enrollees remembered it long after their time there: "The finished carpentry work and the ornamental iron hinges and stuff like that—a man named Burke ran the blacksmith shop. They did all of that there," a boast several enrollees at Garner echoed.[14] The successes of specialty shops were often due to the talents of particular LEMs. Other shops resulted from planners' decisions to make some camps and work sites centers for various

In a makeshift assembly line set in a stand of timber, CCC enrollees and LEMs split logs into the shingles for roofing materials at Bastrop State Park. (TPWD)

Having already completed the wane-edged cladding of Lockhart State Park refectory, enrollees prepared the roof for wooden shingles. (TPWD)

kinds of craftwork. A case in point was the timber mill at Bastrop, which fabricated furniture and shipped it to other park sites around the state. As a former Bastrop enrollee recalled, "The government would buy like a pasture from somebody, and we'd go out there and find some trees that we thought would make some good lumber, cedar lumber. We had a dry kiln over there where we put it in and sawed it up and put it in this dry kiln and kiln dried it. Then we'd take it over to this furniture factory and make furniture out of it for use around in some of these buildings, like chairs and stuff."[15]

As inspectors tour the work site at Bastrop State Park, these CCC men display their decorated interior truss for the refectory. (TPWD)

Indian Lodge at Davis Mountains State Park and the motor court, pump house, and caretaker's residence at nearby Balmorhea all relied on adobe brick. In this ca. 1935 photograph, the CCC enrollees had just removed forms and are preparing to stack the bricks for drying. (NARA, College Park, Maryland)

Camps at Lake Brownwood, Palo Duro Canyon, and Longhorn Cavern also had furniture shops. One enrollee stationed at Longhorn Cavern remembered using cedar and pine for furniture: "I think that's all we had. I think that's all they cut and brought in. See, the logs come out of the park here. They had a mill over there where they cut them up, made the lumber. Then they brought it down to the sawmill where we were building the furniture. We planed it, got it ready to use. Then whatever they wanted to make out of it, that's what we did."[16]

This early mill building at Bastrop served as a carpentry shop. Here, enrollees fashioned furniture, architectural decoration, and even boats. (TPWD)

Enrollees at Palo Duro Canyon State Park with the furniture they constructed on-site. A label on the original photograph, dated January 31, 1935, identifies the wood as native cedar driftwood. (NARA, College Park, Maryland)

Enrollees who learned or demonstrated talent for the building trades received special assignments or assisted LEMs. There are many examples of such specialized work: forged door hinges and handles at Bonham; the architectural moldings at Goliad; the fancy carved walnut mantels in Bastrop's cabins and refectory; as well as the elaborate stone mosaic for the floor of Bastrop's gatehouse. These and other decorative details display the artistic treatment buildings received and testify to the abilities of LEMs and enrollees to execute complex designs.

An unidentified enrollee applies last-minute finishes to an iron chandelier. Most CCC camps needed a blacksmith shop to fashion hardware and lighting fixtures, as well as to repair tools and equipment. (NARA, College Park, Maryland)

An enrollee at Goliad molds clay for a pot to be displayed at the reconstructed mission or at the superintendent's house. His expertise allowed him some respite from the South Texas sun and an opportunity for specialty work. (TPWD)

In 1937, CCC enrollee James Taylor created a bust modeled in clay that would later be carved in walnut and used as a decorative fireplace mantel bracket in the refectory of Bastrop State Park. (TPWD)

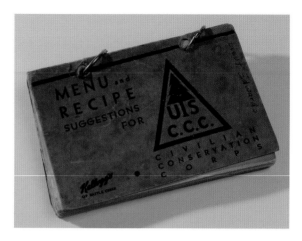

Published by Kellogg's in 1935, this copy of Menu and Recipe Suggestions for the US C.C.C. *belonged to a Lieutenant Edwards. Directions for making ham loaf and American chop suey, seasonal menus for three meals a day, and the nutritional importance of bran were part of the cookbook, which Edwards augmented with his own recipes for various desserts and Italian spaghetti. (TPWD)*

Thanksgiving 1935
Menu

Mixed Sweet Pickles	Green Olives	Hearts of Celery
	Cream of Tomato Soup	
	Roast Turkey	
Cranberry Sauce		Giblet Gravy
	Oyster Dressing	
Snowflake Potatoes		Georgia Candied Yams
Young June Peas		Shrimp Salad
Fruit Salad		Sliced Tomatoes
	Hot Rolls	
Mincemeat Pie		Pumpkin Pie
	Chocolate Layer Cake	
Mixed Nuts		Mixed Candies
	Fruits of the Season	
Fruit Punch		Coffee
Cigars		Cigarettes

Garner State Park's Company 879 enrollees enjoyed a particularly delicious meal in celebration of Thanksgiving that included their choice of after-dinner cigars or cigarettes. (TPWD)

Tables are set for a generous Thanksgiving meal in this barracks-turned-mess-hall at Lampasas State Park in 1933. (#1989/6-9, Don R. Brice Collection, TSLAC)

Food in the Camps

Mealtimes were high points of the day. The food served may not have been of gourmet quality, but as CCC director Robert Fechner described it, it was "the variety that sticks to the ribs," and workers could count on eating regularly. To hungry new enrollees, a breakfast of stewed prunes or scrambled eggs was hearty stuff. Suppers of chicken, steak, beans, rice, potatoes, cheese, and butter were even better. As one put it, "Life in the camp, I would say it was beautiful because we had— when you was out there working on a farm, you didn't know where your next meal was coming from. But when you was in the CC camp, you knew where you were going to get your three hots a day."[17] The telling statistic was that when they first arrived in CCC camps, men typically weighed 145 pounds or less. When they left the camps, however, they were on average 30 pounds heavier.[18]

Education in the Camps

If the CCC had as its sole purposes caring for the employment and physical well-being of several million men during the Depression Era, it might not have gone beyond providing lodging, work, and three square meals a day. But Roosevelt and his CCC officials sought to invest in enrollees' future lives, too. As the CCC took shape, formal educational programs became an integral part of camp life. These programs pursued broad goals of personal growth and development, and they gave purpose and structure to after-work hours in the camps.

In 1940, enrollees of Company 3803 working at Fort Griffin learned the basics of metalworking at nearby Albany Public High School. (NARA, College Park, Maryland)

Educational courses provided key elements of a public school curriculum, enabling enrollees of Company 845 in Beaumont to complete basic requirements for high school graduation in 1935. (NARA, College Park, Maryland)

Enrollees with interest in or talent for painting or drawing could hone their skills in art classes provided in CCC camps. (NARA, College Park, Maryland)

Often conducted in partnership with local schools or businesses, and frequently utilizing moonlighting or unemployed local teachers who were paid by the WPA for their time, evening classes ranged from academic training to social skills. The formal educational programs complemented on-the-job vocational training, and in the case of some subjects like mechanical drawing, radio servicing, and auto mechanics, they expanded enrollees' vocational knowledge. Several of the Texas CCC camps took special pride in these programs, likely prompted by a particularly dedicated educational adviser provided by the Office of Education. Cleburne's camp published illustrated teaching outlines of their own for original courses, in addition to those prepared for all CCC enrollees. At Mother Neff, the men were able to select from twenty-nine classes ranging from elementary school– to college-level courses.[19] Classes in art, music, dancing, and typing helped the men enjoy and master what they pursued during their spare time, whether it was playing in bands and orchestras, taking advantage of books and magazines in camp libraries, publishing camp newspapers, or just socializing.

Recreation in the Camps

The daily routine of the CCC provided discipline, training, and structure. But there was still time for recreation and relaxation. Many of the camps had a hall equipped with pool tables, table tennis, and card tables, as well as a canteen that sold candy and tobacco. After finishing a day's work, enrollees would write letters

Members of Company 3804 spend their spare time shooting pool in the recreation hall at Cleburne State Park. (NARA, College Park, Maryland)

Enrollees at Caddo Lake State Park provide entertainment in their barracks, ca. 1934. (NARA, College Park, Maryland)

Softball was a popular pastime for Company 879 at Garner State Park. (NARA, College Park, Maryland)

to girlfriends or mothers, get haircuts in the camp barbershop, or play board games. Some read in the camp library or listened to the radio. Others escaped evening activities by hiding out in cars in nearby woods or sneaking out to buy alcohol from local bootleggers.

The enrollees engaged in a wide array of activities. They played guitars and sang cowboy songs and held sing-alongs. On weekends there were all-day barbecues and sporting contests, such as softball, boxing, baseball, track, and tennis. Camp teams played one another in region- and district-wide athletic competitions.

Read All About It, in the CCC Paper

While camp papers ran the gamut in quality from amateur to professional, the content was fairly standard and included national news and safety articles mixed with gossip and humor. A regular column in Company 3805's paper titled "Dripping of Eaves," later changed to "Eaves-dropping," recounted overheard conversations, many apocryphal. From Camp 817's *Blue Eagle News* came a column titled "Willy Wonders," in which the author posed questions big and small: "Who said that we're all created equal?" and "What chance has a short-armed man in the mess hall?" Enrollees also showcased their drawings and poetry. Among the most-touted camp publications was Bastrop State Park's *The Pine Bur.*

The Tide of 3805 *camp newspaper from Bartlett, Texas, was known for its art deco illustrations, thanks to the talents of its company's enrollees. (TPWD)*

Events also included spelling bees, essay and arithmetic contests, and extemporaneous speeches.

An activity that bridged the gap between education and recreation was composing and publishing a camp newspaper or newsletter. Stories in them focused on camp antics and achievements, especially athletic victories of enrollees and teams. It was one thing to read *Happy Days*, the national journal of the CCC, or *Chips*, the official information bulletin of the district headquartered at Fort Sam Houston, or *The Roundup* newsletter of the West Texas District. But it was another thing altogether to produce one's own company newspaper and read about close work-mates and friends. Almost one hundred camp newsletters were produced across Texas, ranging from *The Windy Rim* produced in Canyon to *The Mosquito*, hailing from Karnack. The newsletters provided interesting and entertaining glimpses of life in the camps and the feeling of community in them. They included articles about work, health care, education, athletics, social events, religion, and the local community.

Race Relations in the Camps

The experiences of African Americans and Mexican Americans in the camps also involved the routines of long workdays and three daily meals, but sometimes their work assignments and recreational activities differed from those of white enrollees.[20] At least in part, these differences are captured in anecdotal evidence of racial discrimination within CCC companies and camps. Stories survive of racist remarks made by army officers and Forest Service personnel, for example, and if they complained about discriminatory incidents, the victims risked being ignored, disciplined, or transferred.[21] In some instances where African American enrollees found their situations intolerable, they responded by refusing to work and deserting the camps. Photographs showing African Americans posing separately from white enrollees, wearing different uniforms, and huddled far from where officers and mascots are located speak volumes about difficult race relations.

Approximately 250,000 African Americans served in the CCC nationwide, and an estimated 5,000 did so in Texas, where there were twenty-three CCC companies of African Americans. Two of those companies were composed of World War I veterans. When it was conceived, the CCC was intended to be a fully integrated organization with the goal of enlisting African Americans as 10 percent of all enrollees, a proportion that matched that of African Americans in the general population at the time. However, this goal ignored the fact that unemployment and impoverishment among African American men were twice the levels of those of other Americans.[22]

For all its progressive accomplishments, the CCC could not escape its cultural milieu, and in 1935 it was forced to bow to social pressures and segregate its companies of enrollees.[23] Thus, African Americans were not allowed to serve in most supervisory positions, and similar to African Americans in the US military, they were often assigned menial tasks preparing meals in kitchens or serving them to others in dining rooms.[24] It was also the practice to exclude African Americans from educational and other special programs.

This photo of Company 888 enrollees and supervisors who built Mission Tejas State Park was taken in 1934 when CCC companies were still integrated. However, note the spatial separation of the nine African American members from the Anglo enrollees. (TPWD)

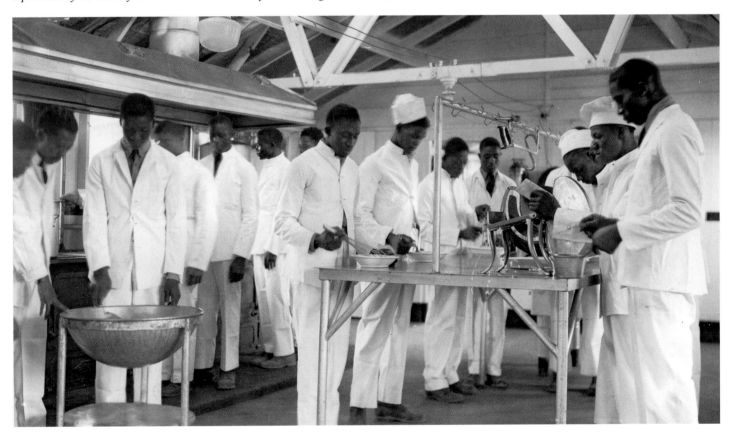

Segregated Company 3801(C), in Waco, Texas, during a cooking class in October 1938. (NARA, College Park, Maryland)

Integrated and Segregated Companies

Even before the CCC instituted a policy of segregating black companies from white companies, some sought subversive ways to make this happen. Dayton Jones, director of the California Emergency Relief Administration, proposed that by assigning African Americans to kitchen duty, they would necessarily eat apart from those whom they served and thus be segregated from white enrollees. Yet the joke may have been on Jones since in segregated units, African American enrollees engaged in all sorts of skilled labor quite apart from cooking meals and cleaning up afterward.

A further irony is the case of Company 1823(CV),* a segregated company forced to move from its initial assignment at Sweetwater's municipal park because of local protests about a group of mature African American men being in the town. Originally an integrated company of two hundred whites and twelve blacks, all World War I veterans, Company 1823(V) became segregated Company 1823(CV) when CCC director Fechner mandated this as national policy. Abilene was the first to welcome Company 1823(CV), recognizing its enrollees' construction skills and relishing the company's singing group at local events. The men likewise enjoyed Abilene's movie theaters, concerts, and other entertainments. Later, other places such as Kerrville, Ottine near Gonzales, and Huntsville embraced the company as a means of gaining a park.

---

* Letters following company numbers indicated that all of the men in a company were veterans (V), African American or "colored" (C), or African American veterans (CV).

Although segregation was not mandated between Anglos and Mexican Americans, oral histories reveal that some informal segregation occurred particularly during leisure activities, such as dances and sports, evidenced by this photograph of Company 879's basketball team comprising solely Mexican American members. (NARA, College Park, Maryland)

After 1935, African Americans in the CCC nationwide were usually placed in all-black companies where they performed work identical to that in white companies—planting trees, fighting fires, constructing parks, and alleviating soil erosion. To the extent that African Americans participated in all aspects of building parks, in Texas and elsewhere, they did so in all-black companies. In Texas, some of these companies encountered vociferous local community opposition to their proximity, and this forced relocating the companies to areas of the state less opposed to their presence. Nevertheless, all-black CCC companies contributed importantly to building the Palo Duro Canyon, Abilene, Daingerfield, Palmetto, Goose Island, and other parks.

For Mexican American enrollees, situations varied. Some camp classes were taught in Spanish, as was a 1934 first-aid class for Company 879 at Fort Davis (Davis Mountains State Park), because Spanish-speaking members constituted more than half of the company. In February 1940, three-quarters of CCC enrollees building a park at Garner were Mexican Americans. Although white workers and Mexican Americans worked side by side at Garner, they lived in segregated barracks and socialized in separate circles.[25] One former white enrollee at Garner recalled, "If they had a dance, the whites stayed away. If the whites had a dance, the Mexicans stayed away." Another white enrollee said he remembered Mexican American

The CCC held dances at their camps like this one in 1933. Residents from the adjacent town were invited, and local bands provided entertainment. (NARA, College Park, Maryland)

company leaders keeping their enrollees "in line," citing an occasion when some Mexican Americans "stuck their heads" into a white dance and a company leader came to get "hold of them."[26] In a time when interracial marriage was scorned and illegal in many states, racial separation certainly occurred in the CCC.

CCC Camps in Communities

As keen as some members of Texas communities were to obtain a CCC camp, others were suspicious of outsiders coming into their locale. But where positive relationships developed between a camp and a local community, a camp's success was assured. By buying supplies from merchants and spending the discretionary five dollars per month on goods and recreation in towns, camps and enrollees became parts of local economies.

Many Texans welcomed enrollees into their homes, hosted events for camps, and donated books to camp libraries. Local church members embraced enrollees who attended worship services, and churches were places where enrollees met and mingled with community residents. Enrollees' attendance at church services reassured local citizens about the strangers in their midst, and churchgoing enrollees were aware this was one way to gain acceptance by the local community.

A Little Socializing

"We had two or three different churches there and I went to church at the Baptist Church and several more of the boys did, too, and we enjoyed that and we got acquainted with the local girls and boys and enjoyed that because I finally got one of 'em, kind of singled her out as my girlfriend."—*Bill Hendryx, Lake Brownwood State Park*

Tell It to the Folks

One good cure for the "blues," or whatever ails you, is writing letters—to your family, your friends or the girl back in your home town. Most boys who come into the CCC maintain regular correspondence with home, keeping their families informed about themselves, their work and their life in camp. This means much to the father or mother back home. Parents feel the absence of the boy quite as much as the boy feels the separation from home. It is a good habit to form—that of writing letters home regularly.

There is much to write about. Parents are interested in hearing about your life in camp and the best means they have of getting this information is through your letters. Mothers are interested in knowing about your food, your clothes and your companions. Fathers are interested in your work, your foremen and the manner of conducting your camp. Small personal experiences a boy may have in camp, which may not seem much to him, may be of great interest to father or mother, or maybe the girl friend. A description of the country around camp, the nearby town where you go on week-ends, the kind of people you meet, all make good "fodder" for letters.

* * *

You will want to know how things are going at home, how your mother is and how your father's work is getting on. You will want to know, perhaps, how Sis is getting on in school or with her new boy friend. You will want to know about brother Johnny. The best way of getting letters FROM home is to write letters TO your home. It doesn't cost much to write letters, but if you cannot afford a three cent stamp, lay in a supply of penny postal cards. They can be a second-best contact with the folks back home who are thinking of you.

Letters written home may form an interesting diary of your activities while in the corps. If written with this in mind they can be doubly valuable, both to the folks at home and to you in the years to come, when you probably will look back upon the CCC as a great experience in your life. Putting your thoughts down on paper in letters also helps you to understand things better, or to get unpleasant things off your mind.

Regular schedules for incoming and outgoing mail are maintained in each camp. Generally, mail is distributed at a certain time, and each enrollee should inform himself of the time when mail leaves camp. Camps use a regular government post office of the nearest or most accessible town.

— 46 —

If You Get Married

If, after you join the CCC, you meet "the girl of your dreams" and you get married, you will not be eligible for re-enrollment in the corps, unless you are a war veteran or are in the overhead group exempted by law. Enrollees who marry after entrance in the CCC are permitted, however, to complete the enrollment period they are serving. War veterans, project assistants and the other exempted overhead (five men per camp) are not disqualified from CCC eligibility by marriage.

— 47 —

Homesickness was common among young enrollees who had never before left home. Orientation handbooks like this one, which all new enrollees received, advised how to cope. The handbooks also informed enrollees about other issues they might encounter while in the corps, including what to do if they met that special someone. (TPWD)

Enrollees no doubt had other sorts of mingling in mind when they attended community dances and visited local theaters. At Daingerfield and other camps, CCC trucks transported local women to the camps for dances that sometimes lasted until well after midnight, before returning the women to town. Town residents were often invited to attend camp entertainments, watch events like boxing and wrestling matches, or see movies shown in camps. Not surprisingly, some enrollees eventually married women living in the local communities, as did some camp officers.[27]

MOTHER

M is for the million things she gave to me.
O means only that she's growing old.
T is for the tears she shed to save me.
H is for her heart of purest gold.
E is for her eyes with love light shining.
R means right and right she'll always be.
Put them all to-gether they spell
MOTHER
A word that means the world to me.

A number of firms manufactured and marketed so-called novelties, like this pillow top, to CCC enrollees. A verse such as this one may appear sentimental to today's viewers but was probably consoling to the mothers whose sons were working far away. (TPWD)

A Different Life

Not all of those in Texas CCC camps were happy to be there. State Parks Board draftsmen and architects in the camps were undoubtedly grateful for the paid work the camps provided them. But some army cavalry soldiers, pulled away from what they loved and had trained for, did not enjoy new roles as CCC "babysitters." More than a few enrollees were homesick. Despite camp facilities and activities, they longed for the familiarity of home. Others resented CCC work practices and camp discipline as harsh and unjust.[28] Homesickness and resentment contributed to desertions.[29] For some the CCC was not a worthwhile experience, and they fled it as soon as they could. But available evidence indicates clearly that for the great majority of enrollees, the CCC was a home away from home and a solution to grave financial hardships.

A family gathered around a CCC-built stone and concrete picnic table at Bastrop State Park in 1965. Some thirty years after Companies 1805 and 1811 had constructed Bastrop and Buescher State Parks, the scene had changed dramatically. Gone were the CCC camps filled with hungry youths recruited by county welfare groups. Instead, young families arrived in station wagons and enjoyed a leisurely game of catch, a cookout, and sliced bread. (TxDOT)

The CCC Legacy's First Half Century

By the early 1940s, many CCC enrollees had completed their time in camps and left their CCC work experiences behind. But on December 7, 1941, the Japanese bombed Pearl Harbor, and the United States declared war against Japan and Germany within the next few days. During the months that followed, former CCC enrollees found themselves wearing new uniforms as members of the US armed forces, into which they quickly enlisted or were soon drafted.

As early as summer 1940, the State Parks Board told the War Department in Washington that park buildings and facilities in Texas would be made available for military use. Governor W. Lee ("Pappy") O'Daniel welcomed the board's offer and turned several parks over to the military for use as training camps.[1] The military soon requested permission to use still other parks for temporary troop staging areas and for troop rest and recreation.

Balmorhea State Park was a popular swimming hole for the military even before the 1940s, as seen here. Drawing from El Paso's Fort Bliss to the west and from Marfa's Fort D. A. Russell, the park accommodated the cavalry, which frequently held maneuvers near Balmorhea. Here, in 1938, Fort Bliss Cavalry Training Camp takes advantage of the pool the CCC built around San Solomon Springs. (TPWD)

In 1939, the cavalry camped at Balmorhea State Park. (U.S. Cavalry Memorial Research Library, Fort Riley, Kansas)

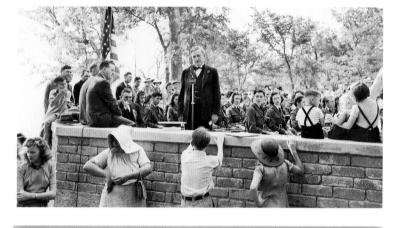

Pat Neff spoke at Fort Parker State Park's opening on May 1, 1941. Frank Quinn is seated to Neff's right in front of the flag. (As published in the May 8, 1941, issue of the Humble Oil Sales Lubricator, *State Parks Board records, TSLAC)*

A picture postcard advertises Huntsville State Park, ca. 1945. (Walker County Historical Commission)

World War II eventually took millions of Americans to Europe and the Pacific. Civilians who remained behind were ready to make sacrifices and do their part in the war effort. They accepted the need to ration goods and commodities, such as gasoline and rubber tires for automobiles. During the summer vacation season of 1943, the *San Antonio Evening News* reminded readers that "the Office of Price Administration holds that a long automobile tour is a luxury which a nation at war cannot afford."[2] And newspapers around Texas, only some of them prompted by the Parks Board, observed that visiting state parks usually involved just short drives, and for this reason parks became highly popular destinations during the war years. Far from forcing the closure or warehousing of CCC parks, wartime spurred their use by many Texans. Newly completed parks became attractive and convenient destinations for recreation.

They Didn't Finish Our Park

The wartime shortages that prevented Texans from traveling long distances also prevented completing the construction of some parks. Building supplies were scarce or at a premium, and the war swept many supervisors and artisans into the military.[3] As Americans, Texans understood the call of national defense, but residents of some communities still felt that promises to construct nearby parks had been broken. They clamored for a dam and lake or for cabins, picnic tables, trails, and park roads promised before the war.

Some South Texas and Hill Country residents wanted all of the planned twenty-six cabins at Garner State Park to be completed. When war broke out, only fourteen had been finished and are all that remain, demonstrating consequences of war shortages that persist to this day.[4] Elsewhere some residents thought that progress in building parks was insufficient and argued that property donated for the parks ought to be returned to donors. A proviso attached to the donation of land at Possum Kingdom called for returning the property to the Brazos River Conservation and Reclamation District if the NPS and State Parks Board failed to initiate park construction. However, a CCC camp had been established there in May 1941, and it remained until July 1942, although this was too little time to execute, much less realize, a full-blown master plan and satisfy all enthusiasts for the park.[5] As at Fort Griffin and Inks Lakes, other parks with approved camps and companies got too late a start or had to stop before implementing the original park plans fully. Communities across Texas regarded plans for nearby parks as assets that had been promised but not delivered, and they sometimes did not fully appreciate the wartime exigencies responsible for these disappointments.

The CCC camp of Company 2888 at Possum Kingdom State Park, 1941–1942. (TPWD)

A picture postcard of the Bastrop swimming pool Bill Walters mailed to his mother in Ruston, Louisiana. He wrote, "We're out in the field on more war games. Brrrr! It is cold!" It was posted on November 5, 1941. (TPWD)

Taken from atop the CCC-built Big Spring State Park, the postcard photo features a panoramic view of the town of Big Spring at the junction of US Highways 80 and 87 between Fort Worth and El Paso. (TPWD)

Despite such difficulties, the steady increase in park attendance that preceded the war flattened only slightly between 1941 and 1945. Communities banded together and used parks, completed or not, as places to gather. Although shorter trips were made, automobile visits to parks continued. Vacationers and soldiers on the move sent their families picture postcards of bustling Texas towns that were blessed with CCC parks, such as Bastrop and Big Spring.

Public Spaces

After the war the popularity of state parks increased further. Because parks amounted to windfalls for communities across Texas, many a town celebrated their completion. Few CCC parks were situated in remote areas; most were located near towns whose residents had known the locally experienced men, CCC enrollees, and those who governed the camps. Local residents had taught classes, supplied goods, and otherwise interacted with camp members. They had monitored the construction of park buildings and had talked about when their park would open. Towns benefited economically from the many visitors coming to "their" parks, and this strengthened local and regional ties to the parks. Unlike attending school and church, going to parks involved no obligations; parks welcomed visitors without demanding anything of them. Their reason for being was simply to provide public spaces in which to enjoy pleasing landscapes, fresh air, and nature's bounty of fish and wildlife and encourage activities that exercised body and mind. Parks made concrete what a planning meeting in 1937 had envisioned, if in mythic terms:

> What is it about State Parks that attracts people? I don't believe that John Average-Citizen consciously thinks of scenic beauty as a vast and glorious heritage that the Good Lord has provided—and yet I think that is one reason why he goes. In Europe the great monuments are manmade—Gothic Cathedrals and Castle[s] on the Rhine. The scenic attractions there have been modified thru the centuries until the primitive has disappeared. Here we still have the blood of the pioneer coursing thru our veins and the trackless plain, the solemn pine forest, and the uninhabited mountain vastness give us a feeling of true patriotism for our native land. The State Parks are first of all set aside to preserve for all time and for all people, areas of statewide scenic, scientific and historic interest.[6]

During the postwar decades parks hosted day-long programs of music, food, and athletic and other competitions. Celebrants enjoyed bathing beauty contests and boating races where there were lakes. On opening day each year whole communities

A program for the July 5, 1937, Independence Day celebration at Meridian State Park lists exhibitions by champion swimmers and dancing until daylight. (Meridian SP, State Parks Board records, TSLAC)

A handbill announces the opening of Balmorhea on June 26–27, 1936, and lists some of the scheduled activities: an appearance by former governor Neff, swimming races, a baseball game, and boat races at Lake Balmorhea, which is no longer part of the state park. (TPWD)

This image captures a 1954 family reunion in the club-house at Lake Brownwood State Park. Originally designed and constructed by the CWA in the early 1930s, CCC Company 849 renovated the building in 1937, involving major modifications of the door and window placement. This room, labeled "Dancing" in the drawing, contains the grand limestone archway, oak floors, exposed ceiling, and original light fixtures. The doors and windows in the background are part of the CCC modifications. (NARA, College Park, Maryland)

Tyler State Park

The June 12, 1938, edition of the Tyler Morning Telegraph *published a photo of a CCC enrollee taking tickets at the ticket booth at Tyler State Park. (Tyler SP, State Parks Board records, TSLAC)*

After a particularly busy weekend celebrating Independence Day, the Tyler Courier-Times *staff cartoonist Sam Nash chastised messy park visitors, July 4, 1939. (Tyler SP, State Parks Board records, TSLAC)*

would turn out to mark the approach of summer, and throughout the year families and groups came for reunions and other festivities. Former CCC enrollees were conspicuous users of parks they helped build, taking enthusiastic part in celebrations of Memorial Day, the Fourth of July, and Labor Day and becoming still more closely involved in the communities near the camps where they had lived. Claude Miller visited Bonham during his 1941 summer vacation and wrote in the park's guestbook, "I helped build this park. Have been away three years. I was pleased to find it so nice."[7] Certain to have audiences, celebrities and entertainment stars also took advantage of the parks to make appearances. For example, Monte Hale, a popular country singer and western film star in the postwar years, visited Kerrville State Park in 1947.[8] So many celebrants converged upon Tyler State Park's July Fourth holiday weekend in 1939 that a cartoonist for the local newspaper rebuked them for their lack of manners.

Carnivals of Concessions

To bring the CCC to Texas, the state had to make two promises: to work with NPS professionals in designing parks and to operate and maintain parks once they were built. The first promise was easier to carry out than the second, but even the first was not without difficulties. The State Parks Board complained frequently about the NPS's tendency to plan parks without the board's input. The abrasions created by this NPS high-handedness were real though thankfully short-lived. Fulfilling the state's promise to operate and maintain parks once they were built was more difficult. The State Parks Board was simply not staffed or funded sufficiently to operate and properly maintain a statewide system of parks. But when the last of the CCC camps closed in early 1942, and when the NPS closed its Austin office that June, the board found itself presiding over a small "empire" of parks nonetheless.

Parks Board members were well-connected business and community leaders, but they were few in number and had only a small staff in Austin to assist them, with no permanent or trained staff in any of the parks. The legislature had required the board to have a "keeper" at each park, principally to perform policing duties. Early park historians noted that "there was now a system of fairly well-developed parks, without sufficient funds for their proper operation." When CCC development of a specific park site ended, the legislature, they continued, made "small appropriations from general revenue to finance the necessary inspection and supervision required of the state in implementing the CCC park development program and to employ caretakers, or park keepers."[9] After the 1942 departure of the CCC and the NPS, the legislature, for the first time in its history, allocated some one hundred thousand dollars to state parks from general revenue, though it parceled this allocation out in small appropriations to specific parks.[10] However, this was hardly enough money to operate and maintain almost fifty parks.

No longer a partner of the NPS or recipient of accompanying federal funds, the Parks Board gave full-time attention to funding operations of the parks that were now its responsibility. In addition to seeking increased funding from the legislature, the board tried innovative ways to raise money. Leasing mineral rights to parklands was one. Leases enabled oil companies using directional drilling to

This February 20, 1941, drawing by J. C. Dolgarn made clear that concessions were part of the planning of some parks, in this case, Blanco State Park. (TSLAC)

SNACK BAR, CLEBURNE STATE PARK, CLEBURNE, TEXAS

This postcard testified to Cleburne State Park's bustling concession business during the 1940s. (TPWD)

tap petroleum reserves beneath parks and then pay royalties on the petroleum extracted. The legislature was persuaded to create and oversee a Special Mineral Fund from which money for parks, together with general revenue appropriations, could be doled out. Optimism about this new source of revenue led the board to predict that general revenue funds might no longer be needed.

Another source of funds was the board's financial arrangement with park keepers who were allowed to augment their small annual stipend through concessions from which the board would receive a portion of the profits. However, the

Named for a rock formation featured at Palo Duro Canyon State Park, the Sad Monkey miniature railroad, a concession venture, took visitors for a short ride and tour of the park. (Palo Duro Canyon SP, State Parks Board records, TSLAC)

profit motive caused some concessionaires to launch enterprises that ran counter to park values and aesthetics. Some installed pinball machines that fell into disuse once their novelty wore off; others provided jukeboxes that were quite popular but also frequently broken. Wanting to bring some order to concessions in the parks, the board entered into a lease agreement with a business concern known as the Palo Duro Corporation to operate concessions in some of the most popular parks, such as Tyler and Bastrop. But the corporation and the sublessees with which it contracted wanted to operate only during the peak summer season when profits would be greatest. When it was seen that year-round concessions were needed, the contract with Palo Duro Corporation was terminated. Leases to other concessionaires proved more satisfactory, for example, a lease to the Schulekoff Corporation to conduct profitable concessions at Longhorn Cavern. That lease, as one board document put it, "proved successful and was continued until the indebtedness against the land was paid off."[11]

Perhaps not surprisingly, "some people complained about the 'Coney Island type' concessions in state parks, which included airplane rides, a western clothes store, passenger boats, fishing barges, and race tracks."[12] The Parks Board defended such concessions because it sorely needed its share of the profits and simply could not operate or maintain the parks without it. But if truth be told, the board could not sustain the parks even with concession revenues, which went into a Special Parks Fund the legislature had established in 1931, the Special Mineral Fund, and small biennial general revenue allotments.[13]

Parks and Politics

By 1945, the State Parks Board was managing forty-five parks, only a few of which had not been constructed by the CCC.[14] However, Weaver H. Baker, chairman

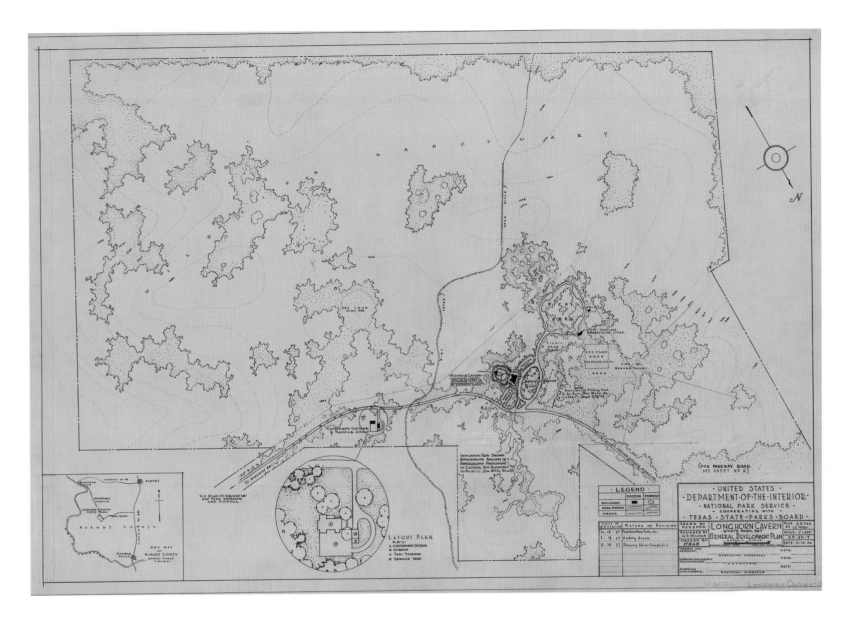

of the powerful State Board of Control, had ideas about using two of the CCC parks—Longhorn Cavern and Inks Lake—for purposes other than public recreation. Functioning primarily as the state's purchasing agency, the State Board of Control had been given, or had grabbed, numerous other duties over the years. Two of them were to manage the state's mental health institution in Austin and manage the historical parks. Baker hit upon the idea of using the recently abandoned CCC barracks at Longhorn Cavern as year-round housing for patients with mental illnesses. After all, he reasoned, the barracks were relatively close to Austin and were lying empty. Placing these patients in them would save the state money.

The General Development Plan of Longhorn Cavern State Park, dated November 16, 1936, shows the CCC camp's location close to the administration building and the entrance to the cavern. (TSLAC)

In addition, Baker proposed leasing land in nearby Inks Lake State Park for cattle grazing. Instead of having to ask the legislature for money, Baker believed he would in these ways be able to return money to the state.

Both parks were located in Burnet County, and more than a few county residents, as well as other Texans, were outraged by Baker's proposals. They pointed out that the original purchase and donations of land were expressly for use as parks. Moreover, although they sympathized with the state's responsibility to care for the mental patients, residents protested that Longhorn Cavern was hardly an optimal location for people with mental infirmities. Possibly some who voiced this opposition did so because they also knew that the population of mental health patients was disproportionately African American, with racial animosity being another reason for outrage.

In any event, the Parks Board understood it was no match for the Board of Control and its well-connected chairman, so the Parks Board acquiesced grudgingly to Baker's proposals. But the legislature then failed to fund a refurbishing of the Longhorn Cavern barracks and Baker's plans died. The controversy, nevertheless, consumed much energy and time and demonstrated how vulnerable state parks were to actions by powerful state officials. It also demonstrated a certain lack of clout and confidence on the part of officials managing the state parks system.

Historical Parks Join the Parks System

In 1949, the legislature ordered a study of the Board of Control's far-flung duties. Both the study and the Board of Control itself recommended that the historical parks under its authority be transferred to the State Parks Board. This would enable the Board of Control to concentrate on core duties and ensure that the parks would be better cared for. Excluding the Alamo, which was entrusted to the Daughters of the Republic of Texas, the historical parks were those at Fannin, Goliad, Gonzales, Refugio (King's), Quitman (Governor Hogg), Lipantitlan, Washington-on-the-Brazos, Acton, and La Grange (Monument Hill). In loose partnership with the Board of Control after 1919, local volunteers and commissions appointed by Texas governors previously managed the parks, but the legislature now placed responsibility for them squarely with the State Parks Board.

The Parks Board already had in its purview Old Fort Parker and Fort Griffin State Park, both of which had benefited from work by the CCC.[15] Erected by a unit of young African American enrollees from Company 3807, Old Fort Parker, made famous by Cynthia Ann Parker's abduction by Indians in 1836, was a reconstruction of the original fort. Fort Griffin, near Albany, had lobbied for a CCC camp beginning in July 1934 and was finally allocated a camp in August 1939 to develop

A ca. 1945 postcard of Fort Griffin State Park picnic area illustrates the limited development of the park by the CCC. (Fort Griffin SP, State Parks Board records, TSLAC)

a 519-acre park and restore ruins of the post–Civil War fort there. With eight historical parks transferred to it from the Board of Control, the State Parks Board now managed a total of fifty-three parks.[16]

Funding and Counting Parks

The legislature knew well enough that a state park system existed and had to be funded. But its allotments of funds to the Parks Board grew ever so slowly, though they did increase in successive biennia to make up for federal funds, assistance, and expertise withdrawn during World War II and not restored when the war ended. To take stock of a system that had grown helter-skelter and of how funds allocated to the Parks Board were being spent, in 1945 the legislature asked a member of its Auditing Committee, Representative W. R. Chambers, to conduct an evaluation. Although suspicious of this intrusion into its affairs, the Parks Board had no choice but to cooperate.

Chambers proved to be a conscientious evaluator, and in his report to the Auditing Committee he complimented the board for its park management. He observed that the number of parks managed by the board in 1945 provided ample recreational outlets for Texans and advised against increasing this number. Indeed, Chambers believed that some smaller and less distinctive parks could be closed and their lands returned to those who had donated them because he found much of the land in some small parks inaccessible and undeveloped, without recreational

Although Frank Quinn resigned as director of the Parks Board and returned to private business, he remained very active in park issues. In 1950, he was instrumental in bringing the National Conference on State Parks to Bastrop State Park. Here, the participants enjoy dinner in the park's refectory. (TPWD)

value or scenic beauty, and with little or no historical significance. In colorful terms, he told the Auditing Committee, "It takes more than a cow pasture or a mesquite-covered hill and an excited chamber of commerce to make a park go!"[17]

There was in fact considerable confusion during the early postwar years about how many state parks actually existed. Writing about the opening of Fort Parker State Park, for example, a journalist asserted there were 30 state parks and 414 roadside parks, which consisted of numerous automobile rest stops donated to former Governor Neff's early State Parks Board.[18] During its two decades of existence, the Parks Board accepted many donations of land for park sites. But only the legislature was empowered to make donations official, and it tended to do this haphazardly. One reason was that deeds for donated lands were sometimes not properly recorded, if recorded at all. Consequently, discrepancies abounded in the legal status of lands intended to be parks, so much so that no one could say with certainty just how many parks existed or were intended.[19] The only certainty was that the majority of clearly recognized parks were and would remain for the next two decades those built by the CCC: more than thirty of the fewer than sixty of the generally recognized state parks. When the public, state leaders, Parks Board members, and most journalists and travel writers referred to state parks during the postwar years, they almost always meant the CCC parks.[20]

"As soon as funds become available"

Sharp criticism of Palo Duro Canyon State Park was leveled by a disgruntled Missourian who camped there with his family in 1955. Writing to the editor of an Amarillo newspaper, he complained, "There is no running water, unless you walk or drive a mile or so to fill up your jug; no toilet facilities, the camp sites were littered with watermelon rinds and other refuse that certainly must have accumulated over several years at least. There was also evidence that horses or cows, or both, had wandered through the campsites." Fleeing to the shelter of "cow cabins" advertised by the park, his family found broken windows, barely hinged doors, animal droppings inside, and "great bottle flies" swarming outside.[21]

The unflappable Palo Duro Canyon State Park manager responded publicly that he had one man to clean all the "developed" areas of the fifteen thousand–acre park and that this man did so once a day, after which he burned the trash collected. The manager opined that the Missouri family had arrived after one of the park's busiest weekends when some twenty-five hundred picnickers had been at the park each day. He added that he had banished cows from the park when he took charge the year before and that only fifteen horses roamed the fifteen thousand acres and were available to rent for horseback rides. The manager conceded that the Cow Camp cabins were in poor condition, but he explained that the park's practice was to replace door locks and windows once a month, and if campers found a lock in disrepair only a couple of weeks after it had been replaced, the park stopped renting that cabin. The manager agreed that the park had too few restrooms and said that constructing more was a high priority "as soon as funds become available."[22]

State Parks Board files were filled with such complaints during the 1950s. Visitors leveled criticisms at parks north and south, east and west, large and small. Their complaints varied in tone from vitriolic to good-natured and helpful. For example, after camping at Daingerfield in 1955, a Michigan family wrote to the State Parks Board on the back of a photo they had taken in the park:

> We are accustomed to camping in the rough and enjoy it, even where there are no toilets, but this place tops them all. I could not help myself from taking these pictures for you. At least the fallen down out-building and rotting tables could be piled up and used for firewood. The grounds sure would look more presentable. The water was excellent, also lighting for good campsites too, but a cleanup would be in order. I sincerely hope this is the only park like it in Texas. Thank you. Arthur Nielsen & Family, Taylor, Michigan.[23]

Frank Quinn, Leader of Texas State Parks Board

It was no coincidence that the occasion of the state audit resulted in Frank Quinn leaving his position as director of the Parks Board. With a stagnant salary, inadequate appropriations for parks, and little control over how the scarce funding was expended, Quinn was frustrated. He rushed to take advantage of the postwar business climate and became general manager of an auto dealership. He nevertheless remained very active in state park matters, promoting and fighting for funding of state parks, and eventually became chairman of the Parks Board. In 1950, five years after resigning as a paid staffer, Quinn served as president of the National Conference on State Parks, an organization based in Washington, D.C., and brought its annual meeting to Bastrop State Park. It was a coup for Texas.

Arthur Nielsen wrote the comments quoted in the text on the reverse of this 1959 photo; he also sent a photo of the picnic table with no top and the campground that had no water, lights, or campsites. (Daingerfield SP, State Parks Board records, TSLAC)

Visitors from Georgia arrive at the entry portal to Bastrop State Park, 1954. (TxDOT)

Fashionably dressed women putt on Bastrop State Park's golf course, ca. 1950. (TxDOT)

The absence of an effective strategy for park maintenance and repairs, lack of a trained workforce, and insufficient funds allocated by successive sessions of the legislature (compared with revenues it made available for other good causes and agencies) meant that Daingerfield and Palo Duro Canyon were hardly the only parks in shabby condition during the 1950s. Despite heavy use and much abuse, visits to state parks continued to increase in number.

Swimmers enjoy a day at Daingerfield State Park, ca. 1950. (TxDOT)

Picnickers at Mathis State Park, now Lake Corpus Christi State Park, take advantage of the many concrete picnic tables to have lunch and play dominoes on a summer day in 1954. (TxDOT)

In 1963, photographer Jack Lewis snapped one family's camping trip at Palo Duro Canyon State Park. (TxDOT)

This cartoon depicts the new opportunities to advertise for tourism and old problems of state parks in need of repair. (Acquisition and development files, State Parks Board records, TSLAC)

Advertising the Parks

As revised in 1876, the Texas Constitution prohibited the state government from spending state funds to advertise the state's resources and attractions. This prohibition probably stemmed from hostility Texans felt toward carpetbaggers during Reconstruction. During the post–World War II years, however, it was increasingly apparent that tourists from outside Texas were spending significant amounts of money in local communities, and not encouraging tourism had real costs. Consequently, in 1957 the 55th Legislature amended the constitution to allow expenditures of state funds for purposes of developing and disseminating information about Texas and its attractions.[24]

In regard to state parks, however, the problem was less a lack of publicity than insufficient state funding for park maintenance. Facilities were too few and most were in poor repair. In a time when summer vacations far from home had become as much a part of American family life as cars and baby carriages, park maintenance did not measure up to what a traveling public expected.

Parks as Mirrors of Society

Texas state parks were not isolated from broad currents and problems in postwar American society. Reflecting generally better wages and greater opportunities for leisure activities, increased visits to parks in Texas mirrored increased visits to national parks, which skyrocketed from 22 million visits in 1946 to 54 million eight years later. However, polio was a national scourge, and during successive polio scares, notably one in 1943 at Tyler State Park, potential park visitors had to be urged not to let fears of polio keep them away. The long and severe drought suffered by the southwestern United States during the late 1940s and early 1950s was also felt in Texas parks. By 1953, for example, the drought was so severe that survival of two prized bison in Palo Duro Canyon State Park was threatened because the park could not afford to purchase hay sufficient to sustain them. Luckily, publicity about the bisons' plight motivated a donor to provide the necessary feed.

Nor were Texas parks isolated from the broad national movement to gain civil rights for African Americans after World War II. Having helped build parks before the war and having performed military service during it, many former CCC enrollees wanted to tour parks where they had earlier lived and worked. But if they were African Americans, they were denied entry or shunted to unattractive park areas. Witness what happened to Millard Fillmore Rutherford, a former CCC enrollee at Fort Parker State Park who was African American and a World War II veteran. Rutherford had proud memories of living and working in the outdoors when he

Company 3807(C) pauses for a photo while constructing the dam at Fort Parker State Park, ca. 1935. (TPWD)

was in the CCC camp at Fort Parker. He remembered how he and fellow enrollees had built a dam to create a park lake for fishing and boating. When Rutherford returned to Mexia after serving in World War II, he married and wanted to take his bride to the park to show her the dam. When they arrived, however, they were told that African Americans were not allowed to enter. As Rutherford later recalled with bitterness, "I could not even show my wife the park I helped build."[25]

From the late 1940s until the Civil Rights Act was passed during the presidency of Lyndon B. Johnson in 1964, racial segregation was prevalent in parks and other public places in Texas. But as the civil rights movement gained momentum, the State Parks Board and discriminatory practices by parks were increasingly under attack.[26] There was, in fact, much variation in the extent of discriminatory practices among the many parks. In general, parks refused African Americans the access whites enjoyed, but the Parks Board had no formal policy governing entry to parks on the basis of race, and it made efforts to discover how its parks were acting in this regard. It asked superintendents if they were experiencing much use of parks by African Americans, and it learned that in the absence of a statewide policy, the treatment of African Americans varied greatly. Some parks had not been visited by African Americans at all; some simply accommodated them with no fuss; still others welcomed some and refused others. "So long as they remain apart" was the usual refrain.

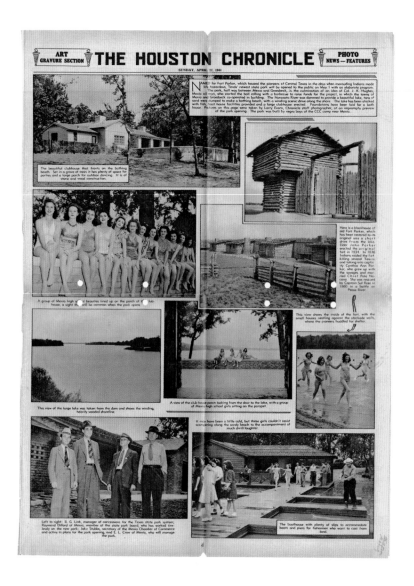

This feature story in the April 27, 1941, Houston Chronicle *showed that no African Americans attended the opening of Fort Parker State Park. However, the newspaper did note that the park was built by the "negro boys of the CCC camp near Mexia." (TSLAC)*

Despite finding that some parks were admitting African Americans and others were not, the board bowed to pressures from outspoken whites unwilling to have African Americans enter parks. The board therefore asked the legislature to fund "separate but equal" facilities in parks or even to fund parallel systems of parks for whites and blacks. Board members were well aware of the legislature's reluctance to allocate significant funds for state parks, and they were no doubt certain that the proposal to create a second park system for use by African Americans had no chance of being funded. In effect, the board threw the hot potato of civil rights in parks into the legislature's hands, asking it to pronounce a general policy.

After the Supreme Court's 1954 decision in *Brown v. Topeka Board of Education*, anticipation spread among whites that all public places would need to accom-

Such an advertisement appearing in TxDOT's annual state guide, ca. 1961, suggests that Texas may have been new at providing large numbers of lodging facilities to accommodate the traveling public. (TPWD)

modate African Americans. The State Parks Board used this prospect to further its efforts to build lodging facilities in the parks, with mixed support from area residents and private lodge owners. By the mid-1950s, in any case, few of the parks were capable of accommodating additional visitors, whether African Americans or others. It was clear to most observers that expanded park accommodations, especially for overnight visitors, were sorely needed. How to provide them in the face of the legislature's chronic underfunding remained a mystery.

Texas parks also mirrored national trends when the State Parks Board announced in 1960 a ten-year program it dubbed Operation 10/70, which it envisioned as the Texas equivalent of Mission 66, a decade-long effort launched by the NPS in 1956 to prepare national parks for 1966, when the Eisenhower administration's target for completing the interstate highway system was to be realized.[27] The NPS saw correctly that the highway system would produce an unprecedented amount of automobile travel by Americans and foreign tourists, including travel to national parks. Consequently, funding and facilities to accommodate greatly increased numbers of visitors, campers, and overnight guests were imperative. It was perhaps not accidental that the Mission 66 moniker jibed with Route 66, the famous highway on which Americans had previously traveled west. Although the State Park Board's Operation 10/70 sounded more like surgery on a bad pair of eyes,

An Idea to Finance State Parks

Governor Allan Shivers authorized the sale of $25 million in bonds to fund improvements, including lodging for park visitors. In order to limit risk, the bonding company required that the lodges proposed at Inks Lake, Atlanta, and Eisenhower be managed by the right kind of operator to assure sufficient revenue to pay off the bonds. But with interest rates high, the Parks Board did the math and realized that the three parks that would have benefited from the bonds would not bring in the revenues needed to pay them off, a deficit that would have to be made up from revenues earned by other parks. The bond company did not think the revenues would ever pay the bonds and refused to finance the deal. The bonds remained unsold.

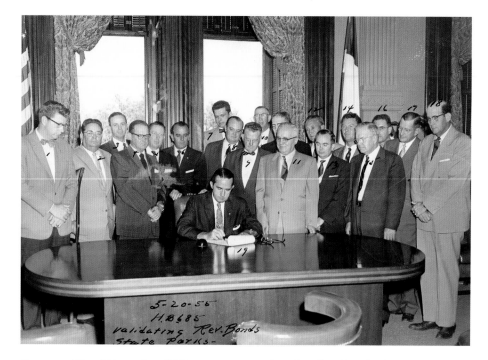

Governor Allan Shivers signed H.B. 685 approving the sale of bonds to fund improvements for state parks on May 20, 1955. Also pictured are legislators and bill supporters from areas of Texas that would benefit from the investment, from 1 to 18: Rep. Harold Kennedy, Marble Falls; Rep. Obie Jones, Austin; Rep. Horace Jackson, Atlanta; Hon. Andrew Howsley, Texas State Parks Board, Albany; Hon. Howard Carney, Atlanta; Hon. Hershel Hanner, Atlanta; Bob Abel, Mgr. CC [Chamber of Commerce?], Atlanta; Hon. Joe Graham, Banker, Atlanta; Frank D. Quinn, Texas State Parks Board chairman, Austin; Homer Knowles, Lumberman, Atlanta; Rep. J. O. Gillham, Brownfield; [number 12 was left blank]; Marvin Hagemeir, Insurance, Atlanta; Mr. Dunn, Burnett; H. H. Galloway, Banker, Burnet; Albert L. Rodgers, Real Estate, Austin; Houston Clinton, Burnet; Burt Debo, Insurance, Burnet. (State Parks Board records, TSLAC)

it was likewise intended to generate funds for improvements to CCC parks, historic sites, and other public spaces under the board's jurisdiction. But as happened with earlier board requests for additional funds, Operation 10/70 went nowhere when the legislature once again refused to increase park funding.

CCC Parks Point the Way

By the early 1960s, the state parks' plight was in sharp focus. The failure of revenue bonds for parks, authorized by Governor Allan Shivers, awakened many to the fact that funding by the legislature and the portion of keeper and caretakers' profits

Indian Lodge at Davis Mountains State Park, 1962.
(Photo by Willis Albarado, TxDOT)

received by parks were grossly insufficient. In 1959, the *Texas Observer* wrote about the pitiful state of affairs in which visitors had to foot the bill for each activity at a park, and it highlighted the severe limitations on the number of employees the Parks Board could hire. To further prove the long-standing needs of parks, supporters had only to point to an ongoing feud at Davis Mountains State Park. The park was situated on land leased to the Parks Board for ninety-nine years, albeit with a proviso that if the land ever ceased to be used as a park, then it would be returned to the lessor. When maintenance of the park's famous Skyline Drive and shelter, picnic tables, and barbecue pits at the drive's top lagged soon after the CCC company that built the park departed, the lessor fenced the park entrance and reclaimed ownership, with a court supporting this action. The standoff persisted until key legislators interceded on behalf of the Parks Board in order to accomplish the needed maintenance at Davis Mountains State Park and Indian Lodge.[28]

Everyone concerned with parks during the early 1960s acknowledged that something had to be done to meet the recreational needs and demands of a growing and increasingly urban and mobile population. The State Parks Board had done its homework and provided a well-researched list of needs for each state park. To study the funding problem, the Texas Research League hired Texas Tech University, which offered an academic degree in park management. The study, like others before it, recommended greater support for repair and maintenance of the

This photograph of Governor John Connally and President Lyndon B. Johnson enjoying a casual drive as their wives sit in the back seat of the convertible suggests their personal friendship, one forged on many shared interests, including a love of Texas lands and the outdoors. (TPWD)

park infrastructures, reliance on professionals rather than caretakers, acquisition of additional public lands, and a culling of the current system as essential to an improved state parks system.

When Governor John Connally took office in 1963, he made good use of the Texas Tech recommendations to set priorities for that year's legislative session. He stated boldly, "We must decide what we want in the way of parks and what it will cost, then provide this service to our people, or not attempt to engage in the activity at all."[29] Seeking a reliable income stream for parks, Connally hit upon the idea of tying park funding to funding for conservation obtained through federal funds totaling more than $26 million per year made available by the Pittman-Robertson and Dingell-Johnson Acts. The federal aid allowed a 75 percent federal match of funds generated by a state tax on hunting and fishing equipment. This prompted Connally to engineer a merger of the State Parks Board with the Texas Game and Fish Commission to form the Texas Parks and Wildlife Department. Although some at the time said the merger had more to do with punishing the Game and Fish Commission for a game warden who had insulted Lyndon B. Johnson, Connally's close ally and friend, it was more likely that Connally's keen love of the outdoors prompted his action.[30]

Under President Johnson, the Land and Water Conservation Act passed by the US Congress in 1964 also made funding available to state and local communities for acquiring, planning, and developing recreational facilities.[31] The new TPWD created a Texas Outdoor Recreation Plan and submitted it to Washington to show how federal funds would be used in Texas and how matching funds would be acquired. The legislature duly authorized park bonds in order to raise the state matching funds, on the assumption that if the bonds raised as much as $75 million, Texas parks would, with the federal matching funds, have $150 million to provide the long-sought safety net for existing parks, as well as money with which to acquire lands for new parks.[32]

To sell the so-called Connally bonds, the legislature allowed state parks to charge an admission fee for the first time. But the authorized one dollar per vehicle hardly covered indebtedness on the bonds, and State Senator Don Kennard had to step in. As his colleague Senator Bob Armstrong recalled, "I remember the day that Don came up with the crazy idea. We were on the Senate floor and he said, 'Why don't we tax cigarettes a penny?' It was brilliant."[33] Supporters of state parks soon spoke enthusiastically about "the cigarette tax" because it gave parks a reliable funding source, taking in about $16 million annually, approximately one-half of the total generated by the tax.

Something else boosted the fortunes of state parks during and after the 1960s: the evolving awareness among lovers of the outdoors—anglers, hunters, and nature

Bonham State Park pavilion became a scene for teens' dances in 1967. (Herman Kelly, TxDOT)

Wildlife, or perhaps the region's scenery, catches the attention of backpackers in Palo Duro Canyon State Park. (Jack Lewis, 1975, TxDOT)

At Palmetto State Park, a guide provides a tour for a family in 1970. (Jack Lewis, TxDOT)

Families enjoy the swimming pool at Abilene State Park. (Jack Lewis, 1976, TxDOT)

Crowds gather at the cavern entrance at Longhorn Cavern State Park. (J. Griffis Smith, 1985, TxDOT)

enthusiasts—of the need to collaborate with one another and with the parks system if prized ecosystems, distinctive land formations, and historic sites were to be preserved. With the Texas Tech study's recommendations as backdrop, this awareness encouraged TPWD to embark on what a recent article calls in retrospect the "golden age" of land acquisition for parks.[34] Land acquired included what became Dinosaur Valley, Fort Richardson, Hueco Tanks, Pedernales Falls, and Guadalupe River State Parks and Historic Sites. Altogether, these and other land acquisitions doubled the number of Texas parks and historic sites, as well as total park acreage.

Swimmers flocked to Blanco State Park's CCC-constructed dam in 2005. (Michael A. Murphy, TxDOT)

Hikers pause to take in the view from Painted Rock at Garner State Park. (J. Griffis Smith, 2001, TxDOT)

View of the canyon from Palo Duro Canyon State Park Visitors' Center. (Stan A. Williams, 2007, TxDOT)

The CCC parks were not eclipsed by this large expansion, however. The experience of partnering to build, manage, and enjoy the CCC parks had prepared Texas for further expansion of the state park system. Because water recreation in state parks was so popular, land for new parks was evaluated for its potential to add swimming, fishing, and boating opportunities to the system of parks. But TPWD naturally continued to accept donations of desirable lands, something that had been done from the time of Governor Pat Neff's early crusade for parkland in the 1920s. Today, TPWD floats bonds to repair parks just as the State Parks Board did to acquire noteworthy CCC parks, such as Longhorn Cavern and Palo Duro Canyon State Park. The basic model for creating parks employed jointly by the State Parks Board and the NPS during the Depression-wracked 1930s has guided Texas state park development ever since.

"It's a dirty job, but . . ."
Spattered in paint, Nola Davis led a team of artists to
refresh the fading wall paintings at the CCC reconstruction
of Mission Nuestra Señora del Espíritu Santo de Zúñiga at
Goliad State Park and Historic Site in 2006. (TPWD)

Preserving the Legacy

That's the wonderful thing about a park; it can be many things to you, it can be anything you want it to be and you don't need to think about the depth of who built this, made this road, built that chimney behind us, but the more you learn about it the more it means to you, the more it becomes part of your own birthright, your legacy, the more you want to go to the next one to see what they did there, too. —JIM STEELY[1]

As 1983 approached, the NPS, many state park systems, CCC alumni groups, and others prepared to celebrate the fiftieth anniversary of the Civilian Conservation Corps. Becoming officially "historic" at fifty, according to criteria of the National Register of Historic Places, the buildings, features, and landscapes of CCC parks became objects of scholars' studies, stewards' enthusiasm, and alumni celebration. During the quarter century since the anniversary, the CCC parks have continued to garner attention, appreciation, renovation, and, of course, wear and tear.

Celebrations of the fiftieth anniversary in 1983 took many forms. Stewards of the national CCC parks produced brochures and pamphlets; organizations to reunite enrollees sprang up or strengthened; at reunions, celebrants swapped stories and shared treasured photographs and artifacts of camp life; they returned home to write reminiscences.

Aware of what this anniversary meant for TPWD's historic properties, a core group of Texas historians and architects launched the first inventory of them. Historic preservationists, professionals employed by TPWD to implement the National Preservation Act of 1966, formed the agency's Historic Sites and Restoration Branch. In 1983, historian Sue Moss directed an initial inventory of CCC parks, and architect Sarah Boykin catalogued each park's features. "Although our group focused on parks acquired for their historical significance," Moss recalls, "we all thought about the NPS architects and the CCC builders—now *that* is the kind of park planning we want to do—planning that will last!"[2] They also set out to analyze the nuts and bolts of CCC buildings to ensure preservation of each park's original design.

The CCC parks in Texas are now more than seventy-five years old, and preserving their legacy is a multifaceted undertaking. This chapter examines some of the facets and seeks to lay the ground for further protection of the legacy as the one hundredth anniversary of the CCC approaches.[3]

Documenting the Legacy

Efforts to document the CCC legacy for the fiftieth anniversary sparked work by TPWD staff to document it further. During years following the anniversary, the TPWD team of preservationists analyzed the design and construction of main CCC buildings, uncovered the origins of designs, and identified people who had planned the parks. TPWD architects inspected CCC park drawings with new

Drawing of custodian's cottage at Longhorn Cavern State Park, by S. C. P. Vosper, dated March 7, 1934. In addition to presenting the elevation, plan, and some construction materials, the drawing includes several notations that provide insight into the design and planning process: "This Cottage is suggested in lieu of three cabins for which $90.00 each has been alloted [sic]. Material cost $270.00," and "Maier affirms this ca[bin] sketch—Nason." (TSLAC)

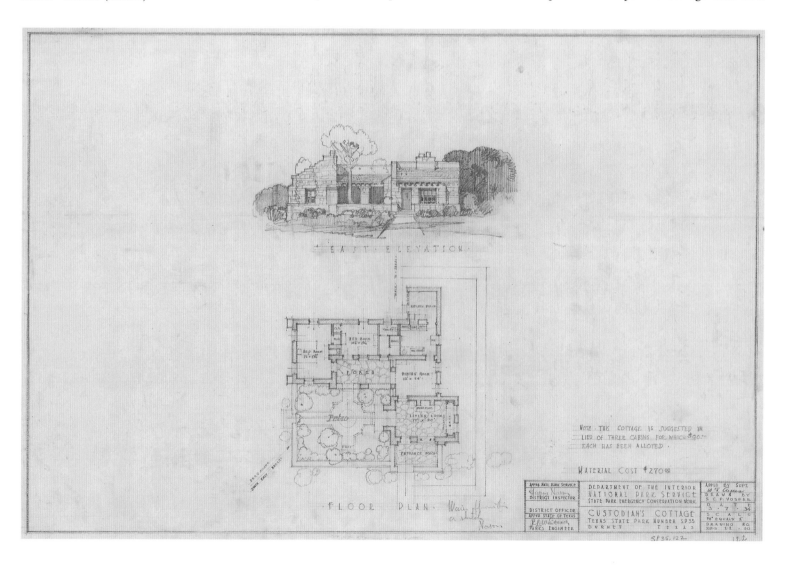

This CCC traveling exhibit was installed at Longhorn Cavern State Park's Administration Building in 1986. (TPWD)

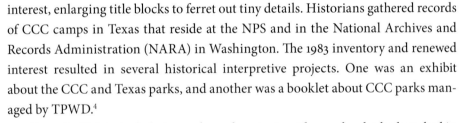

Historical Architect Dennis Cordes lends a hand with oral interviews at the 1998 CCC reunion at Bastrop State Park. (TPWD)

interest, enlarging title blocks to ferret out tiny details. Historians gathered records of CCC camps in Texas that reside at the NPS and in the National Archives and Records Administration (NARA) in Washington. The 1983 inventory and renewed interest resulted in several historical interpretive projects. One was an exhibit about the CCC and Texas parks, and another was a booklet about CCC parks managed by TPWD.[4]

Pursuit of historical photographs and contacts with people who had worked in the CCC led TPWD preservationists to seek out and interview former CCC enrollees who by the 1980s were entering or nearing retirement. The aim was to have these men recall their youthful CCC experiences and the impact the experiences had on their lives. The preservationists found former enrollees eager to recount pranks they had played on one another, what they ate, sports they played, and what it was like to work on park structures. Uniformly, former enrollees expressed surprise and satisfaction to find their contributions were being remembered.

For preservationists who work on what is called historical vernacular architecture, these interviews were memorable experiences. They came face-to-face with men who could speak knowledgeably about how detailed constructions were carried out even though most had been untutored in building trades. Because of the appeal CCC parks have for TPWD staff members, who relish the opportunity to preserve the legacy of the CCC as part of their jobs, this venture in grassroots oral history has continued ever since. Trained in disciplines such as history, architecture, and archeology, TPWD preservationists work with others in the broad field of "resource management," which includes ecologists eager to study how the CCC protected the lands on which it built parks.[5]

Maintaining the Legacy

Appreciation of the CCC parks' distinctive ambience combined with affection for the now frail but jocular men and their rich memories to stimulate much interest in the parks during the 1990s. Efforts to acquire additional knowledge about the overall condition and resources of each park were undertaken. This involved archival research, archeological and architectural analysis, and close attention to things that make a park work, such as culverts, cabins, fireplaces, and picnic tables.[6] All features were incorporated into a wider inventory, assessed, and scheduled for maintenance and repair. This work went hand in hand with a shift in the National Register Program, administered by the NPS, from noting single buildings as historically and architecturally significant to noting entire districts and landscapes—in other words, all of the features that contribute to parks.[7]

A state parks survey team fans out to locate archeological sites at parks, including CCC parks. (TPWD)

A Force Account team member studies a damaged scupper at Goliad State Park and Historic Site in January 1991. (TPWD)

Force Account team members create a mold to cast a new scupper for the Goliad repair, 1991. (TPWD)

A Force Account team member replaces the scupper at Goliad, 1991. (TPWD)

The task of maintaining the buildings and features put in place by the CCC now so long ago rests with each park's staff. But TPWD also has what is called a Force Account consisting of small groups of expert craftsmen who travel across the state regularly to repair and maintain CCC park structures. The Force Account crews work in concert with park and regional staffs, as well as with architects and planners located in Austin.

Force Account team members repair the stone and wooden refectory at Buescher State Park in 1989. (TPWD)

Force Account team members conduct masonry repairs on a Buescher State Park bridge in 1989. (TPWD)

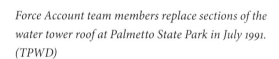

Force Account team members replace sections of the water tower roof at Palmetto State Park in July 1991. (TPWD)

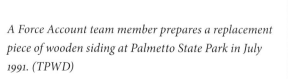

A Force Account team member prepares a replacement piece of wooden siding at Palmetto State Park in July 1991. (TPWD)

A member of the Force Account team uses a lift to replace damaged siding on the water tower at Palmetto State Park in 1991. Company 886 had originally built a coursed sandstone base for the water tower and topped it with vertical split-log siding that resembled a raised palisade. In 1946, the tank was encased in a steel frame, and the vertical siding was replaced with horizontal cedar clapboards. (TPWD)

With responsibility for cyclical maintenance and major repairs to the Bonham State Park boathouse—a building approaching eighty years of age—TPWD completed extensive repairs in 1995, which included roof replacement, post repairs, and a new coat of paint. (TPWD)

Men associated with Company 3807(C) attended their first reunion at the park in 1993. Here, they pose next to a historical marker commemorating the CCC work. Gathering annually with family and friends at the park they built, the men share stories about the CCC and their lives. (TPWD)

A CCC reunion at Garner State Park, 2005. (TPWD)

Spreading the Legacy

The pace of TPWD efforts to preserve the CCC legacy quickened with the CCC's seventieth anniversary in 2003 and its seventy-fifth in 2008. A main reason has been awareness that former enrollees, who were part of "the greatest generation" of Americans, are fast disappearing from the scene. In addition, new technologies and preservation techniques are changing processes of collection and preservation. Scanning historical photographs and other documents is today much easier and faster. Video recorders now lend themselves to nontechnical users, and Internet Web sites make videos accessible to wide audiences. Likewise, transferring oral

Garner State Park has new wayside exhibits that include the story of the CCC. Funded in part by the Friends of Garner, the park has received new trail signs and other interpretive information. Erin McClelland served as project manager and worked with Museumscapes of Dallas, 2011. (TPWD)

TPWD executive director Carter Smith and CCC exhibit designer Drew Patterson celebrate the completion of a new traveling exhibit in 2008. (TPWD)

history tapes to digital modes facilitates preservation of sound tracks for use by future researchers and in public programs.

These technological innovations make it possible to provide a greater variety of interpretive media to visitors before and when they arrive at parks. Historic photographs illustrate new wayside exhibits; video interviews with former enrollees are part of mobile applications; and new exhibits about CCC parks also reflect many of these innovations.[8] Web sites containing information about work in progress at parks are created whenever funding allows.

Funded by Humanities Texas' Linden Heck Howell Texas History Grant, this Web site, *A New Deal for Texas Parks*, is geared to teachers and students and can be accessed via TPWD's Web site. (TPWD)

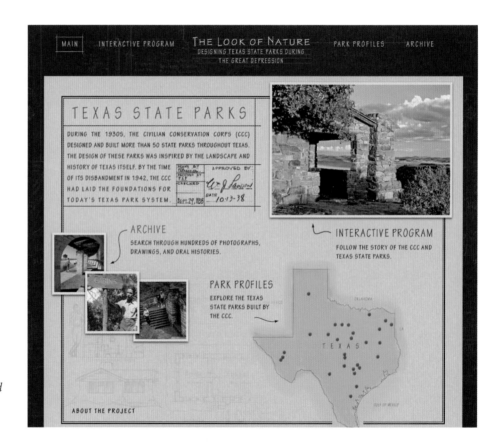

The Look of Nature: Designing Texas State Parks during the Great Depression, www.texascccparks. org, completed in 2009, was funded by TPWD; Hillcrest Foundation, founded by Mrs. W. W. Caruth Sr.; National Endowment for the Humanities; and Roy and Christine Sturgis Educational and Charitable Trust.

Providing for the Future

Regardless of technological changes, the goal of preserving artistic works and historic resources in the CCC state parks does not change. It involves showing how park designs resulting from the NPS-CCC collaboration during the 1930s grew from American ideas about beauty, nature, and recreation that flourished before World War II. And it involves telling the rich, complex, and little-known stories of the Hispanic and African American, as well as some Anglo, workers who built the parks in racially integrated and segregated CCC companies. The TPWD seeks to educate visitors of all ages about these historic aspects of the CCC parks while also targeting today's younger and computer-literate audiences. The overall aim is to ensure that all visitors, including "virtual" ones, recognize the CCC parks' appealing designs and features. Underlying this is the belief that with recognition comes stewardship and a readiness to draw on superior historical designs to build future environments.

Above left: Indian Lodge at Davis Mountains State Park. Above: Before sunrise at Indian Lodge in Davis Mountains State Park. Left: Room interior at Indian Lodge in Davis Mountains State Park. (all: John B. Chandler, TPWD)

Goliad State Park and Historic Site. (John B. Chandler, TPWD)

Chapel interior at Goliad State Park and Historic Site.
(John B. Chandler, TPWD)

TPWD artist Rudy Garcia restores the original luster to a corbel in the chapel of the 1930s
CCC reconstruction of Mission Nuestra Señora del Espíritu Santo de Zúñiga, Goliad State
Park and Historic Site, 2006. (TPWD)

The concession building was part of a major repair project at Daingerfield State Park. The park hosted an open house on October 15, 2011. (Bryan Frazier, TPWD)

TPWD's Force Account team rehabilitated cabins at Garner State Park during 2011–2012. (Dave Bell, TPWD)

Daingerfield State Park boathouse was also rehabilitated during the 2011 major repair. (Bryan Frazier, TPWD)

Risking the Legacy

Although some who visit Texas CCC parks do so simply because they are close to home, many others frequent the parks because of their pleasing scale, picturesque settings, and the quality craftsmanship of their facilities. Indeed, some visitors reserve specific stone and wood cabins for stays in the parks, distinctive refectories for family reunions, and solid stone tables for picnics. Many of the CCC parks are alternatives to municipal and county parks that are more limited in size and lack large open spaces. The larger state parks, especially those close to urban populations, provide much-needed green space for healthy activities and psychological renewal. In all these respects, CCC parks meet needs for outdoor recreation, rest, and adventure.

The CCC built three of what have consistently been among the state parks generating the highest revenue: Inks Lake, Garner, and Balmorhea. All three attract large groups who keep returning, as well as many travelers visiting for the first time. The size; access to boating, fishing, and water recreation at Inks Lake; and its proximity to the populations around Austin and the Hill Country help explain its

Campers and boaters at Inks Lake State Park. (TPWD)

In April 2003 Texas Highways *magazine noted that "in the 1930s workers from the Civilian Conservation Corps started Garner's famous summer dance party for their own entertainment. Today, the dance (held every night in the summer) is perhaps the best-loved event in Uvalde County. Many a romance has blossomed here beneath the stars." (J. Griffis Smith, 2002, TxDOT; Maxine Mays, "Let's Go to Garner!,"* Texas Highways, *p. 21)*

Teenagers swing into the Frio River at Garner State Park in 1970. (John Suhrstedt, TxDOT)

Balmorhea State Park attracts large crowds that tax its ability to accommodate all those who drive long distances to enjoy its cool waters and overnight lodging. (Kevin Stillman, 2003, TxDOT)

A picnic, a bike ride, a hike on the natural trail, a canoe ride, and a tour of historical exhibits are all possible at Goliad State Park and Historic Site. (TPWD)

profitability. Likewise, Garner draws numbers often exceeding its capacity because Central and South Texas residents regard it with much fondness as a traditionally family-oriented, entertaining place offering delights for teenagers. Balmorhea breaks the mold in many ways because it is in far West Texas and distant from major population centers. It is a desert wetland situated at the headspring in a system of springs that has attracted people for centuries. Some seventy-five years ago when CCC enrollees constructed Balmorhea, they probably didn't realize they were building a recreational hub to which a quarter million visitors would eventually flock each year. Then as now, Balmorhea is *the* jumping off point for automobile tourists to the Davis Mountains and gateway to far West Texas for many Americans.

There is widespread agreement among Americans about preserving *national park* buildings and sites constructed by the CCC. But it sometimes seems there is less agreement about preserving buildings and landscapes of *state CCC parks*, including those in Texas. Showing that the Texas parks are superior examples of CCC park design, scholars plead for greater efforts to preserve them. In an authoritative book, *Presenting Nature: The Historic Landscape Design of the National Park Service: 1916 to 1942* (1993), Linda Flint McClelland concentrated more on the CCC parks in Texas than on those in any other state. She highlighted Bastrop, Palo Duro Canyon, and Palmetto State Parks as glowing examples of CCC building and landscape design concepts. When successfully nominating Bastrop State Park for designation as a National Historic Landmark, the historian and landscape architect Ethan Carr depicted Bastrop as a beautiful instance of "the general policies for state park development promulgated by Conrad Wirth and Herbert Maier at the

Canoeists enjoy the calm water and fall foliage at Caddo Lake State Park. (Richard Reynolds, 1986, TxDOT)

Lonnie Dickey relaxes in a hammock at Bastrop State Park. (Bill Reaves, 1989, TxDOT)

In 2006, TPWD restored Indian Lodge's appearance, room configurations, and landscape to their original CCC designs. TPWD engineer and historic preservation specialist Doug Porter adds the final touches by installing reproductions of original 1935 exterior light fixtures. (TPWD)

National Park Service . . . [containing] outstanding and seminal examples of the 'NPS Rustic' style as adapted to state park development beginning in 1933."[9]

It is difficult to imagine that the rich CCC legacy in Texas may one day be forgotten. Yet it is at risk. Despite efforts to secure funds for maintaining and improving parks, and despite the popularity and recreational needs parks fulfill, their beautiful and naturalistically designed buildings and landscapes are deteriorating. If this is not reversed, the loss will be great and irretrievable. Knowing this, TPWD asks each session of the Texas legislature to make increased funding for CCC and other parks and historic sites a high priority so the backlog of needed repairs to CCC buildings and parks can be erased. The State Parks Division of TPWD also asks Texans of all types to appreciate more strongly the distinctiveness and historical significance of *their* parks. This request is not simply in order to preserve beautiful buildings and settings or even to capture what CCC workers contributed to Texas. Preserving the CCC legacy is these things, but at its heart it is ensuring that parks continue to enrich Texans' and all visitors' lives.

"What has always drawn me to CCC buildings, more than anything else, is how accessible they feel. They're not regal palaces built for the super rich or postmodern architectural experiments. They're warm, inviting places that were built by everyday people for everyday people. Their materials are familiar and the facades are inviting. These are buildings that welcome people and complement their surroundings at the same time."
—Erin McClelland, cultural historian

Twilight view of clubhouse at Lake Brownwood State Park. (Kevin Stillman, 2000, TxDOT)

"The harmony between CCC buildings and their natural surroundings brings me great joy. When I see one, I am reminded that the built environment and nature can exist together without one taking away something from another. It's quite peaceful, in a way. I am always reminded of this relationship when I sit in the lookout shelter at Davis Mountains State Park. Even though I am in a man-made structure that frames a beautiful view, I feel close to nature. From just looking at these structures, it's obvious that great thought, care, and craftsmanship went into designing and building them, but when you know the story of the CCC, the experience has new meaning." —Sarah Helwick Lisle, historic preservation professional

The overlook at the top of Skyline Drive in Davis Mountains State Park, 1999. (TPWD)

"I enjoy the individual rustic charm of each CCC structure or feature—the fireplaces, lighting fixtures, wood furnishings, native building materials, and other details—that makes each structure unique. This character is further enhanced by the location of the architecture in picturesque natural settings, such as woods, mountains, or rivers, in such a way that the natural and man-made features do not so much compete with each other as they complement one another. Indeed, it is the ability to look out on the scenic landscape through the window of a CCC cabin, lodge, or other building that often highlights my stay in CCC lodging." —TIM ROBERTS, archeologist

"The structural forms are simple and the lines are clean. You can look at a building and see through the eyes of the architects; and you know that they knew how gravity and environmental forces flow through the frame to the ground. They made beauty by exposing major framing elements while they shaped beams, rafter ends, and carved column capitals." —DOUG PORTER, structural engineer

Members of the West family look out over Bastrop State Park. (Stan A. Williams, 2010, TxDOT)

"CCC structures are rugged, not rustic. Since they are situated in parkland, the visitor usually enjoys peace, calmness, and comfort. When I look at the architectural details, I do not see rock, metal, or wood; instead, I see the hands at work creating it." —NOLA DAVIS, muralist and artist

A view into the canyon from the Palo Duro Canyon State Park Visitors' Center. (TPWD)

"The CCC created outstanding buildings using the simplest of construction methods. The two main skills needed for repair and maintenance are carpentry and masonry. However, the main ingredient in care of these buildings is respect for what they represent and provide." —DOUG PORTER, structural engineer

"Being able to see the chisel marks on a two hundred-pound stone is impressive. I've had the opportunity to visit with some of the men, who once worked in these parks, at CCC reunions held at Bastrop State Park. I enjoy listening to their stories of camp life. To them, it was just life. They were glad to join the CCC, not to be honored for their work, but to feed their families and learn a lifelong skill." —Todd McClanahan, regional director and superintendent of Bastrop and Buescher State Parks

Bastrop State Park refectory. (Bill Reaves, 1989, TxDOT)

Palmetto State Park Refectory, ca. 1937. (TxDOT)

"I have seen the refectory flooded five times, and once in the 1998 flood the only part of the structure that was not submerged underwater was the peak of the roof. How can a building withstand this type of abuse and not have significant damage? The park staff comes in after a flood, power washes all of the mud out, and we are back up and running the next weekend. The proof is in the pudding. CCC structures are so well built that they will stand the test of time for many more generations to come. Now in saying that, I must add that the cost to repair such structure is enormous because one, the techniques that were used in doing the work must be replicated; two, cost of materials is high; and three, you need skilled labor to reproduce this kind of work." —Todd Imboden, superintendent of Palmetto State Park

"CCC structures are now at least seventy years old. They were made in a different time with different concerns than construction today. The designers included details, and the CCCers spent time to fabricate those small details with an eye toward building things to last. But without the means to maintain, they will not last. That is our dilemma."
—Tom Fisher, superintendent of Fort Parker State Park

"The important thing is to take care of what we have and keep them in good order. If we do, they'll continue to last a very, very long time and maintain their historical integrity."
—WALT DABNEY, National Park Service and Texas State Parks professional

"We are going to all the CCC parks because they all have this unique architecture style; once you know the CCC 'style,' you can pick it out anywhere." —ANONYMOUS entry in Fort Parker State Park guestbook

This woodcut illustration stresses the importance of fire management as part of the work that the CCC enrollees undertook. In some parks, especially those in timbered East Texas, they constructed fire towers and water towers to facilitate the work. ("Woodsmanship for the Civilian Conservation Corps," 1938, p. 14, Civilian Conservation Corps files, State Parks Board records, TSLAC)

Inferno at Bastrop
on Labor Day Weekend 2011

BASTROP—An erratic, persistent forest and brush fire, which spread over some 30,000 acres, was extinguished Thursday, after CCC-trained fire fighters had battled the conflagration for three to four days.

This and other reports of a fire in Bastrop State Park and the fight by CCC workers to extinguish it appeared in area newspapers on March 12, 1942. The builders of the park, CCC Companies 1805 and 1811, had vacated the park in October 1939.[1] Although they were not present to fight the 1942 fire, other CCC companies were nearby, most important, a company at the Lake Austin CCC camp. Superintendent C. L. Turner was therefore able to send forty-two workers to fight, day and night, "the aggravating flame, which would be put under control and then flare up again elsewhere." Exhausted by this struggle, the Lake Austin enrollees were relieved by one hundred more sent from the CCC camp at Seguin. Bastrop mayor Will J. Rogers (unrelated to his famous namesake) praised the young men and observed, "If it had not been for these CCC boys, Bastrop state park would have burned up."[2]

Some seventy years later, on Labor Day weekend 2011, the park and much of Bastrop County were again subjected to a fierce fire, which was sparked by electric power lines blown down in strong winds and which quickly became an inferno as a consequence of many months of unrelieved drought. This time, TPWD's Wildland Fire Team, part of the State Parks Division, heeded desperate calls for help.

Established by TPWD in 2005, the Wildland Fire Team consists of 160 men and women who operate or manage state parks. In addition to their primary jobs, these professionals study best practices in conservation management. To prevent fires, they regularly use controlled fires to reduce fuel loads—masses of combustible material—that help restore park habitats and protect park infrastructures. Following guidelines of the National Wildfire Coordinating Group (NWCG), team members meet training requirements for each level in the team's organization—firefighter, squad boss, single resource boss, burn boss, and so on.

In this photo taken only weeks before the fire, Megan, a swimming instructor from Friends of the Pines, exchanges a high-five with student Bella Simpson in the Bastrop swimming pool, Bastrop State Park. (Photo by Randall Maxwell, June 11, 2011, TxDOT)

A fire team member looks at the flames from behind the wheel of her truck. (TPWD)

The flames engulf a stand of the Lost Pines on Labor Day weekend 2011. (Chase Fountain, TPWD)

In 2011, the fire team was led by the appropriately named Jeff Sparks, and on Labor Day weekend Sparks and his family were enjoying a day with his parents at Lake Palestine in Northeast Texas. A cell phone call informed him a fire was burning at Bastrop State Park. Located a four-hour drive from Bastrop, Sparks noted that this was the fortieth such call he had received during the 2011 summer and that such calls usually reported small fires quickly extinguished by firefighting crews in local fire departments. Still, he loaded up his fire team equipment, called Austin to dispatch additional firefighters, and began driving southeast on State Highway 21 toward Bastrop. When Sparks reached the intersection with US Highway 290, still several miles from Bastrop, he proceeded through a police roadblock and almost immediately saw giant flames illuminating the night sky. Driving toward them, Sparks soon saw houses, barns, and fences burning, but no firefighters. "It was literally like driving into a war zone," he later recalled.[3]

Not among those who panic easily, Sparks and his firefighters are trained in "situational awareness," which means they size up what is going on around them and look for potential problems, safety options, and escape routes.[4] Scanning the Bastrop situation, Sparks thought this fire, having already burned longer than most, might well be one of an entirely different magnitude. After making a brief stop at the park headquarters, he and other fire leaders went straight to the fire incident command center in downtown Bastrop to determine TPWD's role in fighting the fire. He quickly realized that his fire team would be part of a massive

The Rockhouse fire threatened the Davis Mountains State Park and Indian Lodge during April 2011. (Chase Fountain, TPWD)

Looking west toward Indian Lodge from Skyline Drive. (Chase Fountain, TPWD)

As the Rockhouse fire damage was being assessed, a wildfire broke out at another CCC park, Possum Kingdom State Park. (Chase Fountain, TPWD)

effort to quell a fire that by then engulfed thirty-four thousand acres. Assigned to Division "G," his team had the mission of protecting the park area extending from Highway 21 in the north to Highway 71 in the south.

State Parks Maintenance Manager Robert Crossman was at home in his Austin apartment when he received a call about the fire. Although not a fire team member, he realized immediately that logistical support for the team would be

Aftermath of wildfire at Possum Kingdom State Park. (Chase Fountain, TPWD)

Adrienne Brammer, the assistant office manager at McKinney Falls State Park, also works as a member of the Wildland Fire Team. (Chase Fountain, TPWD)

A TPWD photographer captured this view of the smoldering night fire still threatening the Bastrop pines. (Chase Fountain, TPWD)

crucial. Driving rapidly toward the Bastrop park's western and as yet unburnt side, Crossman did not see the flames and burning structures Jeff Sparks saw when he drove toward the park's northeastern side. Once at the park, Crossman learned his job was to be incident commander, thus enabling Sparks and his team to concentrate on fire suppression. As Crossman later summarized it, "Incident commander carries the mission of the jurisdiction that he or she works for and translates that into a coordinated effort on the ground and in a legal manner carries out that mission."[5] It was his responsibility to marshal and coordinate TPWD staff experts on public safety, public information, planning, operations, logistics, and financial support. A man of calm demeanor, Crossman set about avoiding a situation in which chaos could easily take over.

"We started at 7:00 Monday morning at Bastrop administrative office," Crossman recalled, "but eventually the smoke and fire got so bad in the east that we had to go to the golf course near the park entrance portal to get behind the wind from north to south. There we set up in Jeff's trailer. That was our office and it has a generator."[6] They started looking for water trucks, wanting to soak an area that would serve as an island in the burning park. But all available water tenders—trucks with water-hauling capability—were already committed to saving people's homes, so Crossman and Sparks had to get their own trucks.

They called Carter Smith, TPWD executive director, who agreed that the construction industry might have trucks and other equipment that could be of help. In

When water was available, the fire team kept the roofs of the historic buildings wetted down at Bastrop State Park. Here the team douses the NYA mill, currently used as a sign shop and warehouse. (Chase Fountain, TPWD)

Smoke swirls around the refectory, pool, bathhouse, and pergola at Bastrop State Park. (Chase Fountain, TPWD)

An aerial photograph in Bastrop State Park shows that even a narrow park road can act as a firebreak. (Chase Fountain, TPWD)

The fire team managed to keep the fire at bay even as smoke looms over one of the CCC-built cabins at Bastrop State Park. (Chase Fountain, TPWD)

fact, some construction firms were already offering to help. Not wanting to over-look any and all sources of assistance, Crossman later credited several such companies for pitching in: Ranger Excavation, Jimmy Evans Construction Contractors, and Niece Equipment. He recalled that "Mr. Niece himself was driving a truck for us. And TPW Commission chair, T. Dan Friedkin of Comanche Ranch, sent trucks all the way from Carrizo Springs." The company constructing a Formula

One racetrack in Austin loaned TPWD state-of-the-art equipment not being used during that holiday weekend. All of this equipment was used to soak areas around park buildings and roofs because, as Crossman discovered, "There was no municipal water around the cabins in the park and Aqua Utilities, the municipal water source, lost water as each Bastrop house burned."[7]

Assisting owners of burning homes was a strong need, but as Sparks commented, "Some of us have training in structural protection, but we do not go into burning buildings."[8] His team nevertheless helped save several houses in residential areas adjacent to the park, especially those located on street corners where there was defensible space and relatively little brush, fuel load, leaf litter, trash, and the like. Crossman added, "We did have engines out fighting fires of homes when we could spare them, and we believed that by stopping the fire and saving the park, we could keep the fire from moving west and taking out the businesses and homes there."[9]

Although chances of saving adjacent houses were good if the fire in the park could be contained, the fire team soon found that the fire was highly unpredictable and exhibited a strange "fire behavior." Unlike most fires this one did not "lie down" at night when the temperature cooled, humidity increased, and the sun's radiant heat disappeared. Crossman remembers several close calls involving "blowups" where a typical fire would have "laid down." The first blowup was around 11:30 on Labor Day night, and it happened very near what had been the CCC barracks.

The Bastrop fire exhibited unusual "behavior" by burning hot during the night when temperatures were cooler. (Chase Fountain, TPWD)

Many partners brought in critical fire equipment and firefighters that allowed the Wildland Fire Team to focus on its mission to save Bastrop State Park. (Chase Fountain, TPWD)

A thin patch of green encircles a cabin, illustrating just how close the fire got to the CCC building in Bastrop State Park. (TPWD)

Jeff Sparks rests during the Bastrop fire. (TPWD)

A second was in the same place a few hours later. Crossman described the inferno this way: "We had a sustained crown fire when three hundred– to four hundred–foot flames blow upwards and fire gets in tops of trees and burns along the top. That is when you get fiery sparks that pop and get pulled into an updraft and then fall down on the roofs of buildings. There is a huge roaring sound from embers on the ground being sucked up and sprayed all over."[10]

TPWD had earlier conducted controlled burns at the park, and had it not done so, the Labor Day weekend fire would have been still more intense and long lasting. When asked if fire team members were aware of the enormous public attention the Bastrop fire was receiving, one said, "I knew it when CNN was at the morning briefing."[11] Another said he realized how much national attention the fire was getting when a Type 1 team arrived, explaining that Type 1 incident management teams are the most skilled and experienced in the United States and provide assistance in large-scale hazardous events. Throughout the terrible weekend, TPWD staffs who were not involved in fighting the fire were glued to radios, TVs, and the Internet, because they did not want the precious park and its buildings to burn: Not *those* historic buildings! Not on *our* watch! And in the end, the buildings were saved.

The wooden roof of the overlook will be replaced in Bastrop State Park. A second overlook suffered similar damage. A building's remote location made some structures particularly difficult to protect. (TPWD)

This undated sketch of the overlook is part of the collection of Norfleet Bone, landscape architect for Bastrop State Park. (TPWD)

Having made it clear that the first priority was people's safety, Carter Smith was overjoyed by the fire team's valiant work and gratified by the outpouring of public and private support for TPWD. The well-trained fire team members were relieved that most of their equipment remained intact and ready for use against future fires. There were disappointments over the loss of several vehicles, a number of nonhistoric park structures, and some park records. And with most of the famed Lost Pines burned to the ground, what remained of the forest was not a pretty sight. Yet the lost vehicles and structures can be replaced, and, as ecologists assure, the forest will regenerate, as it did after the fire in 1942. In the meantime, visitors to Bastrop State Park will be able to see plants and wildlife that would ordinarily not be observable in a prefire closed canopy pine forest or other mature forest.

Although shock about the Bastrop inferno will eventually recede, Robert Crossman will always remember how the Type 1 team and firefighters from other parts of the agency came into the park once the fire was more than 50 percent contained to hold meetings and just get out of their trucks and walk around: "They

Fire damage to Houston toad habitat. (TPWD)

Other disappointments included damage to nonhistoric park facilities, Houston toad habitat, and the Lost Pines in Bastrop. (TPWD)

Fire damage to the Lost Pines in Bastrop State Park. (TPWD)

would drive up to the buildings, look up at those wooden shake roofs, and shake their heads. They were impressed. That was high praise." Sparks agreed with Crossman: "As wildfires go, it was a terrible one. People would have been glued to the news even if the park was not a National Historic Landmark, and others would have been interested exactly because it is a National Historic Landmark. *It has been preserved as it was built.*"[12]

New growth began within a few weeks. Photographer John B. Chandler documented both the aftermath of the fire and the possibility for optimism. (TPWD)

Some photographers found beauty amid the destruction. (John B. Chandler, TPWD)

Members of the TPWD Wildland Fire Team, TPWD logistical support team, and volunteers posed here for a group photo. (TPWD)

After some hard work on a warm day, CCC enrollees, LEMs, supervisors, and a US Army officer pose for an informal group photo. These individuals helped build the park that many helped protect on Labor Day weekend 2011. (TPWD)

Zachary and Mason McClanahan skip stones on Bastrop State Park Lake.
(Photo by Jamie McClanahan)

David Riskind, TPWD's natural resources director, commented, "It's as simple as this—if we had not had our fire team, then we would not have the historic buildings."[13] Perhaps the last word should be given to Todd McClanahan, regional director and superintendent of Bastrop and Buescher State Parks:

With the recent wildfires at Bastrop State Park, I've learned to appreciate these historic structures even more. Knowing just how close we came to losing them forever forces me to admire their beauty with a different perspective. They are so much more than historic buildings; they are historic treasures, which I hope someday my two sons will visit and reflect back on the days of their youth when they lived and played in two of the most important state parks in Texas.[14]

Park Profiles

Approach to Recreation Center, Abilene State Park, Abilene, Texas

Concession building stairway, Abilene State Park, postcard, ca. 1933–1934. (TPWD)

Abilene State Park

Location: Taylor County, near Buffalo Gap and Tuscola, FM 89 to Park Road 32
Dates of CCC activity: 1933–1935
CCC companies: 1823(V) and 1823(CV)
CCC construction: Concession building, swimming pool, two pool shelters, pergolas, water tower, stone pump house, stone seats and picnic tables, round table, and fireplaces. Entrance portals and culverts were lost when Park Road 32 was widened.

Park description: Appearing as verdant woodlands among the low limestone hills of north-central Texas' Callahan Divide, Abilene State Park and its attendant groves of oak, elm, and pecan trees sit along Elm Creek and Lake Abilene. The 529-acre park was developed in several stages: fall of 1933 through September 1934; and

June–September 1935—by two distinct CCC companies—one a mixed-race unit of World War I veterans, and the other an all-black veterans' group. Working with native and local materials, such as limestone and red Permian sandstone, these mature men crafted the concession building's high masonry arches and the pool shelter's pyramidal roofs, designs reminiscent of classic Romanesque architecture. The many cut red-sandstone features—visible on structures as diverse as picnic tables and pergolas—were the vision of Texas architects David Castle of Abilene and Olin Boese and F. W. Digby-Roberts of the State Parks Board's Central Design Office in Austin, whose efforts were funded by the NPS.

Balmorhea State Park

Location: Reeves County, in Toyahville, State Highway 17 at Park Road 30
Dates of CCC activity: 1934–1940
CCC company: 1856
CCC construction: Park Road 30, entrance portals, concession building, bathhouses, cabins (San Solomon Courts), pergolas, shelters, pool, pump house, fences, retaining walls, vehicle and footbridges, pool drain conduit, and caretaker's residence.

Park description: Long an important resource, San Solomon Springs was likely visited by Spanish explorer Antonio de Espejo in 1583. Centuries later, settlers arrived in the arid region, built irrigation ditches, and began farming. In the early twentieth century, engineer and manager E. D. Balcom joined with investors H. R. Morrow, Joe Rhea, and John Rhea to form an irrigation company and in the process gave the town its name (Bal-mor-rhea). Seeing the headwaters of San Solomon Springs as an attractive location for a park, the State Parks Board acquired the land in 1934. The next year, the CCC began construction of a huge double-winged swimming pool at those headwaters.

Using local limestone and adobe bricks, the enrollees, largely area residents, soon completed roads, buildings, bridges, and irrigation conduits throughout the 43-acre park. Architect William G. Wuehrman led a team of architects that included Olin Boese, Paul E. Pressler, George T. Patrick, and F. W. Digby-Roberts through the planning and design phases. They were funded by the NPS and employed by the State Parks Board. Among the notable buildings are the caretaker's residence and San Solomon Courts. A paean to early automobile travelers on US Highway 290, the courts were distinctive one-story, red tile–roofed, white-plastered, adobe brick cabins that had garages in each of the eighteen units. Soon after Company 1856 left in January 1940, Balmorhea State Park had become both a center for travelers touring the region by car and a gateway stop for those heading to the Davis Mountains.

Pool at San Solomon Springs, Balmorhea State Park. (Photo by J. Griffis Smith, 2005, TxDOT)

Refectory at Bastrop State Park, ca. 1941. (TPWD)

Bastrop State Park

Location: Bastrop County, 1 mile east of Bastrop, State Highway 21 to Park Road 1A

Dates of CCC activity: 1933–1939

CCC companies: 1805 and 1811

CCC and other New Deal construction: Entrance portals, Park Road 1, stone curbing, fencing, culverts, scenic overlooks, stone tables and seats, picnic fire pits, amphitheater, campground shelter, water fountains, refectory, group picnic pavilion, custodian's dwelling (currently a cabin), helper's quarters, group latrine (later a cabin, currently storage), additional cabins, golf pro shop and associated golf shop (currently the "Caddyshack" and storage), restrooms, and pump house (no longer in use). The keeper's residence and storage were designed but not built. The swimming pool, bathhouse, and pool shelter are the work of the WPA; the maintenance building was built by the NYA (currently the State Parks Sign Shop).

Park description: Easily one of the most popular and beautifully rendered parks in Texas and beyond, 6,500+-acre Bastrop State Park revolves around the "Lost Pines" of Central Texas, a seventy-square-mile western outlier of pine and oak woodland. The two hundred–strong CCC Company 1805 arrived in 1933, and the two hundred enrollees of Company 1811 arrived in 1934. While the men worked hard to leave the impression that their efforts had little impact on the natural resources of the area, the workers did harvest Bastrop County timber and quarried nearby sandstone to construct the park's many rustic-style structures. Architect Arthur Fehr, who directed most of the CCC work at the park, embraced the design principles of the NPS, which emphasized harmony with the surrounding landscape. The superb walnut, oak, cedar, and pine woodwork on the refectory, including a massive beamed ceiling, along with the fourteen distinctive indigenous cabins artfully nestled within the park's loblolly pine forest, enhance rather than compete with the natural setting.

Two other Depression-era groups, the NYA and the WPA, contributed to the park's many features and structures. The NYA built and used the maintenance building in 1940 to construct furniture and fittings for CCC parks in Texas, including Bastrop. The WPA built both the swimming pool and the original nine-hole golf course as separate projects under the auspices of the State Parks Board. The dam and lake predate the park.

Rock retaining wall at Big Spring State Park, ca. 1990. (TPWD)

Big Spring State Park

Location: Howard County, within city limits of Big Spring, west on FM 700 to Scenic Drive

Dates of CCC activity: 1934–1935 (1927, State Parks Board)*

CCC company: 1857

CCC construction: Entrance portals, Park Road 8, culverts, bridges, concession building (currently park offices), keeper's dwelling, stone pavilion, restrooms, picnic tables, stone steps, and retaining walls. An amphitheater was designed and started but not completed. A stone pump house and a water tank topped by a roof garden were designed but not built.

*Already in State Parks Board inventory when the CCC arrived.

Park description: Centuries ago plentiful spring water amid the arid Texas plains began attracting visitors—Native Americans and Spanish explorers alike—to the majestic Scenic Mountain. During the Great Depression, CCC Company 1857 (described by NPS superintendent Thompson Richardson as "poor but fine boys") transformed some 300 acres of rough country into a state park gem. Quarrying native limestone from the park itself, the CCC enrollees followed the designs of engineer V. J. Eckelkamp, architect Joseph Dodge, and landscape architect Harry Newton, constructing the residence and concession buildings as well as the open-air group pavilion, restrooms, and picnic tables.

Most spectacular of all are the design and construction of the three-mile Park Road 8 scenic loop, often referred to as the Roman Road. The lane spirals up around the mountain to the 2,811-foot-high summit, giving visitors grand views of West Texas plains along the way. Lined by immense hand-dressed stone blocks, the road and native limestone structures fit impressively within the area's backdrop of mesquite, shin oak, and redberry juniper.

Dam and wading pool, Blanco State Park, ca. 2000. (TPWD)

Blanco State Park

Location: Blanco County, on the southern part of the city of Blanco at US Highway 281 and Park Road 24

Dates of CCC activity: 1933–1934

CCC company: 854

CCC construction: Park Road 23, culverts and bridges, retaining wall and steps, stone walks, stone dams, picnic tables, rock seats, benches, picnic table and bench combinations, camp stoves, rock wall, concession house–café (currently a maintenance building), concession building (currently the group pavilion), and pump house (no longer in use). The custodian's cabin burned in 1941 (replacement in a similar style was designed but not built; the current structure dates from the 1980s and does not resemble 1930s-era design). The entrance portals, wells, and latrine no longer exist.

Park description: The park stretches along the banks and terraces of the Blanco River. The riparian habitat includes native and introduced plants and a variety of buildings, structures, and features, all of stone. Town Creek flows into the river near the east end of the park and is spanned by a graceful, one-lane bridge built by the CCC just south of the park's original 1933 entrance (closed due to the realignment of US Highway 281, which necessitated an alternate approach to the park). Park Road 23 takes visitors by park headquarters before reaching day-use features, including the grandest building in the park: the pavilion, which has stone walks and stairs leading to the river, and a terrace and benches from which to view the river. CCC-built picnic table and bench units, freestanding benches, and camp stoves sit on both sides of the river. The majority seat four to eight people, but two elongated versions, aligned end to end, stretch a startling seventy feet. When viewed from either short end, these so-called barbecue tables appear as one vast open-air banquet table, suitable for an al fresco feast. Another distinctive feature of the park is a stone chair, or throne, located above the campground; it once allowed a sitter expansive views of the park and the river, but today dense woods block these views.

Among the earliest Texas parks improved by the CCC, and designed by project architects and planners C. T. Fohl, A. N. Hanson, L. A. Schmidt, Paul R. Roesle, and Olin Boese, Blanco State Park's limestone and timber buildings, stone dams, and low-water bridge all date from a single eleven-month bivouac in 1933 and 1934.

Bonham State Park

Location: Fannin County, 3.5 miles south and east of Bonham, State Highway 78 to FM 271 to Park Road 24

Dates of CCC activity: 1933–1936

CCC company: 894

CCC construction: Entrance portal, concession building (currently the park headquarters and storage facility), waterfront storage building (currently the boathouse), lakeside pavilion, picnic tables, barbecue pits, water fountains, footbridge, and culverts. The water tower, currently in disrepair, is closed to the public.

Boathouse and pier, Bonham State Park, 2008. (John B. Chandler, TPWD)

Park description: The 261-acre Bonham State Park falls within the northern extent of the Blackland Prairie, an area marked by grasslands interspersed with woodlands, near the Oklahoma border. The CCC developed the park, landscaping the rocky, hilly terrain for erosion control and recreational purposes and constructing an earthen dam to impound a 65-acre lake. Politically significant at the time of its development was the proximity of the park to Bonham, hometown of powerful Democratic congressman Sam Rayburn, who became Speaker of the House in 1940. Composed primarily of Oklahoma enrollees, CCC Company 894 constructed buildings of local cream-colored limestone and eastern red cedar, working under supervision of Bonham architect Joe C. Lair and San Antonio architect William C. Caldwell. The overall design exhibits a rustic style.

Buescher State Park

Location: Bastrop County, 2.5 miles northwest of Smithville, State Highway 71 to FM 153 to Park Road 1

Dates of CCC activity: 1933, 1939 (1927, State Parks Board)

CCC companies: 1805 and 1811

CCC construction: Entrance portals, Park Road 1, road curbs, vehicular bridge, concession building, shelter, water fountains, stone fence, hiking trail, concrete tables, earthen dam and spillway, tool house, pump house/water tower, and "Aztec-style" settee, chair, armchair, and sofa. A keeper's house and a contact station were designed but not built; instead, the CCC remodeled the tool house and the pump house into a residence compound in 1937.

Caretaker's cottage and pump house designed by Arthur Fehr, Buescher State Park, 2008. (TPWD)

Park description: A historic route connecting San Antonio de Bexar with Spanish missions in East Texas, El Camino Real (King's Highway) once ran near the area of Buescher State Park. During the Great Depression, CCC Companies 1805 and 1811 improved Buescher (named Smithville State Park prior to 1933) as a sister park to the far more ambitious undertaking at nearby Bastrop State Park and connected the two via a scenic park road through the "Lost Pines."

At some 1,017 acres, Buescher State Park shares with Bastrop State Park the aesthetic goal of blending in with the landscape's rolling hills and pine forests. Architect Arthur Fehr relied on the area's rough stone and hardwood timber when he drew the designs for the park's facilities, which center on the picturesque 30-acre lake.

Caddo Lake State Park

Location: Harrison County, 1 mile north of Karnack, State Highway 43 to FM 2198 to Park Road 2
Dates of CCC activity: 1933, 1937 (1927, State Parks Board)
CCC companies: 889 and 857
CCC construction: Portals, Park Road 2, horse and foot trails, shelter house, boathouse, cabins, concession building (currently the group recreation hall), picnic sites, culverts, vehicular bridges, and well house. The pavilion, latrines, and some picnic facilities are no longer in use. Lookout towers and firebreaks were designed but not constructed.

Park description: The rich history of Caddo Lake stretches back many centuries, the diverse natural habitat playing host to myriad plants and wildlife. And as the

Caddo discovered in the eighteenth and nineteenth centuries, the region's wetlands, forests, and floodplains provided bountiful opportunities for hunting and foraging.

Beginning with a small plot of donated parkland in 1927, the state in 1929 and 1931 designated the entire lakebed as state parkland. From its freshwater marshes, backwater swamps, and majestic moss-festooned bald cypress, Caddo Lake provided plenty of inspiration for CCC enrollees in Companies 889 and 857 in the 1930s, who proceeded to construct landscape-friendly structures.

The park roads at Caddo were planned by NPS-funded designers and landscape architects, notably Joe W. Westbrook and Fred R. Carpenter, whom the State Parks Board employed; CCC enrollees implemented their designs. The concession building and guest cabins were likewise collaborations. The park-building partners of the US Army, State Parks Board, NPS, and CCC undertook an experiment as work at the park drew to a close: converting the temporary barracks and mess hall to park facilities that would allow long-term use. The resulting structures—nine large cabins and a recreation hall, improved with pine, oak, and hickory harvested from the area's upland forest and plenty of native iron ore for the foundations, walls, and fireplaces—harmonize with the natural landscape.

Log cabin, Caddo Lake State Park, 2008. (John B. Chandler, TPWD)

Cleburne State Park

Location: Johnson County, 10 miles southwest of Cleburne, State Highway 67 to Park Road 21

Dates of CCC activity: 1935–1940

CCC company: 3804

CCC and other New Deal construction: Portals, entry bridge, Park Road 21, earthen dam and rock spillway, caretaker's dwelling, garage and truck shed, water tower/pump house, culverts, and table and bench combinations. The boathouse and boat dock were designed but not built. Bathhouse and piping (water and sewer system) were completed subsequently by WPA laborers.

Park description: Situated in the Prairies and Lakes region south of Fort Worth, the area around densely wooded Cleburne State Park attracted a number of Native American groups for centuries before the region was permanently settled by European and Anglo-Americans soon after the American Civil War. Juniper, oak, elm, walnut, mesquite, redbud, cottonwood, sycamore, ash, and sumac trees cover the area's white rocky hills, but it is the beautiful valley of natural springs that eventually stamped Cleburne as a picturesque setting for a park.

Like many parks built by the CCC, Cleburne State Park centers on a water feature—a large lake. Constructed with difficulty and plenty of trial and error,

Color-tinted photograph of the portal at Cleburne State Park, ca. 1945. (TPWD)

the small earthen dam and impressive three-level masonry spillway were finally brought to completion. The undertaking, which fell under the auspices of the NPS, consumed an inordinate amount of time and labor, which likely explains the company's failure to make substantial progress on other planned structures. However, the enrollees were able to complete another major project, the three-mile-long scenic park road. In 1940, Company 3804 was disbanded. And a bathhouse, designed by George T. Patrick, Paul E. Pressler, and R. J. Hammond, did win approval for construction, but only at the end of the CCC era. A cooperative effort between several original designers, now working for the State Parks Board, and the WPA made sure that the building was completed in 1944. Since the 1940s, several buildings have fallen into disrepair, notably the bathhouse, and have been replaced.

Daingerfield State Park

Location: Morris County, 2 miles east of Daingerfield, State Highway 49 to Park Road 17

Dates of CCC activity: 1935–1938, 1939–1940

CCC companies: 2891 and 1801(C)

CCC construction: Entrance sign, boathouse, fishermen's barracks, concession building/bathhouse, dam, Lake Daingerfield (originally called Little Pine Lake), retaining walls, culverts, steps, trails, horse trails, parking curbs, scenic road, "Aztec-style" chairs and tables, and cedar benches. Plans also called for several cab-

Lake Daingerfield and boathouse, Daingerfield State Park, 2008. (John B. Chandler, TPWD)

ins (two were built) and a keeper's cottage, which was not constructed (although NPS buildings may have been adapted as a residence).

Park description: Daingerfield State Park is located in an area historically associated with agriculture, iron ore, and timberlands. Currently, the area is valued for its dense pine and hardwood forests, elements that provide a pastoral setting for this 501-acre park. Two CCC companies—2891, a white unit, and 1801, an African American unit—developed the park from 1935 to 1939. Both companies used local timber and stone as well as concrete to construct distinctive features and worked under the supervision of LEMs and planners, including architect J. Reginald Gunn and landscape architect Calvert Swing Winsborough.

Development of 80-acre Lake Daingerfield, the focal point of the park, dominated much of the early efforts. As it began to take shape, designers finalized plans for associated architectural features that took advantage of the site's hilly terrain, landscaped peninsula, and open beach area. They also maximized scenic vistas, traffic flow, and recreational access.

Davis Mountains State Park

Location: Jeff Davis County, 4 miles northwest of Fort Davis, State Highway 17 to State Highway 118 north to Park Road 3
Dates of CCC activity: 1933–1935, 1940–1942
CCC companies: 879, 881, and 1856

View from the scenic overlook, Davis Mountains State Park, 2009. (John B. Chandler, TPWD)

CCC construction: Skyline Drive, overlook shelter, two mess halls (both adobe; one used by CCC as recreation hall for a short time, currently a residence; the other currently storage), stone picnic tables, stone fireplaces, stone steps, and latrine. See also the profile for Indian Lodge.

Park description: An extensive mountain range provides the setting for one of the most majestic of the state parks and one of the earliest CCC projects in Texas. The Texas legislature specifically directed the new State Parks Board in 1923 to investigate the Davis Mountains for a major destination park to attract both overland motorists and train travelers from nearby Marfa and Alpine. But the State Parks Board failed to obtain land donations or appropriations. Then in 1927 the legislature instructed the State Highway Department to build the Davis Mountains State Park Highway on donated right-of-way, now the Davis Mountains Scenic Loop (State Highways 118 and 166). The new byway construction created much -needed jobs for the region and in the 1930s facilitated construction of McDonald Observatory by the University of Texas on Mount Locke. But by 1933, the Great Depression had so devastated the local ranching economy that landowners at last agreed to donate the initial 560 acres for a state park in Keesey Canyon, along the highway toward Mount Locke. The NPS then assisted the design, and the CCC built inside the park a five-mile scenic road, carved in switchbacks, ascending to the top of the ridge between Hospital and Keesey Canyons. From this ridge, visitors enjoy breathtaking panoramas, including a view of the nineteenth-century military installation Fort Davis, which lent the adjacent valley town its name, and McDonald Observatory on a mountaintop to the north. Likely designed by William C. Caldwell, the stone overlook shelter at the top resembles the prototype that NPS architect Herbert Maier designed in 1924 for Yosemite National Park, right down to the "picture window" framing a fabulous view for mountain trekkers resting inside the shelter.

Combination building on Lake Springfield, Fort Parker State Park, postcard, ca. 1945. (Fort Parker SP, State Parks Board records, TSLAC)

Fort Parker State Park

Location: Limestone County, 7 miles south of Mexia and 6 miles north of Groesbeck, State Highway 14 to Park Road 28
Dates of CCC activity: 1935–1942
CCC company: 3807(C)
CCC construction: Entrance portals, Park Road 28, curbs and culverts, infirmary (currently the park headquarters), caretaker's dwelling, combination building, dam and concrete spillway, picnic table and bench combinations, water fountains, and bathhouse (currently the open pavilion). WPA proposed and designed a group of cabins, but they were not built during this period.

Park description: Fort Parker State Park is located near the 1936 Texas Centennial project where the CCC helped construct a replica of the Parker stockade from which Cynthia Ann Parker was kidnapped during a Comanche raid in May 1836. They followed the designs of numerous planners, architects, and landscape architects working for the NPS and the State Parks Board. Among them were George T. Patrick, Ben R. Chambers, Jay T. Dunlap, I. Gelber, and Donald D. Obert.

The men in Company 3807, sons of African American area sharecroppers, also laid down one of the most striking and ambitious of all CCC projects: an impressive

423-foot limestone and concrete dam across the Navasota River, impounding 750-acre Lake Springfield. The rigorous work involved blasting; breaking and hauling rock for cement; digging out the dam footings, spillway, and wing walks; and pouring cement. Most of the work was done by hand, digging with pickaxes and shovels and hauling rocks and cement in "Georgia buggies," deep wheelbarrows with two wheels. The CCC Camp Mexia had its own sawmill and limestone quarry, at which the men prepared the timber and secured the rock used in the buildings, structures, and features. Ironically, the park's service area was established on the site of the ruins of Springfield, a mid-nineteenth-century African American community, and after completion of the work at Fort Parker State Park, African Americans were barred from visiting the park, a practice that remained in place until the 1960s.

Frio River dam, Garner State Park, ca. 2005. (TPWD)

Garner State Park

Location: Uvalde County, 8 miles north of Concan, US Highway 83 to FM 1050 to Park Road 29

Dates of CCC activity: 1935–1941

CCC company: 879

CCC construction: Park roads, culverts, combination building (including the dance terrace; currently the pavilion), keeper's lodge with service court, stables, horse trails, foot trails, picnic tables and benches, fourteen overnight cabins (as many as fifty were considered in the planning stages), office building, storage house, pump house and water well, entrance portals (at the now-abandoned original entrance from US Highway 83), and a blacksmith shop. The novel idea of a roller-skating rink failed to get past the proposal stage.

Park description: With its deep canyons, crystal-clear Frio River, and limestone cliffs providing an inviting setting, the spacious 1,419-acre Garner State Park (named for John Nance Garner, Uvalde resident, longtime congressman and vice president from 1933 to 1940), has proven to be one of the most popular parks in the state. The trails along the lush river valley attract numerous hikers. Additionally, attending the summertime Saturday-night dances in the pavilion has long been de rigueur for generations of visitors.

The combination building, designed by architect John H. Morris and beautifully finished with a colorful encaustic-tiled floor, is made of native limestone and hewn bald cypress and offers breathtaking views from its perch overlooking the Frio. Although that structure remains a nexus for the park decades later, the other CCC contributions—buildings, landscape features, and furniture fashioned of cedar, cypress, oak, ash, and other native materials—are also worthy of note.

Goliad State Park

Location: Goliad County, a quarter mile south of Goliad, US Highways 183 and 77A to Park Road 6
Dates of CCC activity: 1935–1941 (1931, State Parks Board)
CCC company: 3822(V)
CCC construction: Reconstruction: Mission Nuestra Señora del Espíritu Santo de Zúñiga, including the church, granary, cloister, and workshop. New construction: Museum (currently the park headquarters), furniture and decorative metalwork, Park Road 6, culverts, picnic tables, and the custodian's group. The CCC latrine is no longer in use. A wooden entrance sign no longer exists at the park, and a combination building was designed but not built.

Park description: "Remember Goliad!" was the cry of the soldiers at San Jacinto, bespeaking the symbolic role of the events here during the Texas Revolution. In 1836, the Mexican army under José de Urrea defeated James W. Fannin's Goliad command in the Battle of Coleto Creek and, after marching the survivors to nearby La Bahia Presidio, executed more than four hundred men, including Fannin. Around the Goliad County area, especially at the nearby Mission Nuestra Señora del Espíritu Santo de Zúñiga, are remnants of the past that continue to have great meaning for many twenty-first-century Texans.

Mission Nuestra Señora del Espíritu Santo de Zúñiga, Goliad State Park and Historic Site, 2006. (John B. Chandler, TPWD)

During the 1930s, after research into the history, archeology, and architecture of Spanish missions throughout northern Mexico and Texas, the NPS-funded architects Samuel C. P. Vosper and Raiford L. Stripling, along with archeologist Roland Beard, launched a reconstruction of the mission structures. They interpreted Spanish design skillfully, if rather freely. With guidance from these park planners CCC Company 3822, composed entirely of older war veterans, set up camp in the area and focused their efforts on the reconstruction of the eighteenth-century Spanish mission, using stone from the site and a nearby quarry to accomplish their work. The men also lodged the many artifacts unearthed during the archeological investigations in the park's newly established museum.

Vosper and Stripling's subsequent works, including design of the nearby Goliad Memorial Auditorium and the Fannin Battlefield Memorial, both built with Texas Centennial funding, continued to emphasize the area's distinctive historic legacy.

Combination building, Goose Island State Park, ca. 1935. (NARA)

Goose Island State Park

Location: Aransas County, 10 miles northeast of Rockport, State Highway 35 to Park Road 13

Dates of CCC activity: 1934–1935 (1931, State Parks Board)

CCC companies: 1801 and 1801(C) (April–September 1935)

CCC construction: Entrance portal, concession building (currently the recreation hall), picnic units, beachside roads, bridges, camp shelters with fireplaces, tables and benches (fifteen planned but not constructed), and drainage systems.

Park description: CCC Company 1801, originally a mixed-race company, performed initial development work on Goose Island State Park during two six-month periods in 1934 and 1935. The park, bordered by St. Charles and Aransas Bays and sitting on the Lamar Peninsula along the Texas coastline, was subject to extensive CCC work in clearing undergrowth, planting trees, and caring for "Big Tree," an ancient coastal live oak.

Using local materials, the CCC team, led by principal architects George T. Patrick and Thomas B. Thompson, constructed a concession building made of "shellcrete"—blocks cast from oyster shell—to form the walls and arches. They also improved an existing road that became Park Road 13 and access roads on the 307-acre park, paving them with crushed oyster shells. They finished the park's picnic areas in a suitably "tropical" manner, with thatched roofs of palmetto leaves.

Company 1801 endured harsh treatment and tragedy after the United States reconfigured its formerly "mixed" enrollment to an all African American camp on April 1, 1935. Nearby communities objected, taking their complaints all the way to Vice President John Nance Garner. In June, following a murder associated with the camp, the US Army quickly transferred Company 1801 to soil conservation work at Fort Sam Houston in San Antonio. The incident's aftermath and high-level attention resulted in an absolute racial-segregation policy for the CCC nationally. Henceforth, all black enrollees served in their states of residence; whites (and Latinos) could serve anywhere in the nation. All state governors were charged with ensuring local community cooperation with future assignments of the African American companies, and if no standard work assignments could be found for these companies, they were sent to US Army posts such as Fort Sam Houston and Fort Bliss (El Paso).

Huntsville State Park

Location: Walker County, 6 miles southwest of Huntsville, Interstate 45 (exit 109) to Park Road 40
Dates of CCC activity: 1933–1937; 1937–1942
CCC companies: 873 and 1827; 1823(CV)
CCC and other New Deal construction: Earthen dam, combination building (currently the lodge), boathouse, swimming platform, stone culverts, picnic areas, Lakeshore Road, bridge, stone road curbing, well, water-intake structure, and frame pump house. The proposed bathhouse and cabins were not constructed.

Park description: Huntsville State Park, located within the rolling hills of Sam Houston National Forest, is part of the East Texas Piney Woods region that marks the western limits of the Southern Pine Belt. In response to the depletion of local natural resources in the early twentieth century caused by extensive timber production and the lack of conservation measures, members of CCC Company

Combination building, Huntsville State Park, 2008. (TPWD)

1823 reforested the land through plantings of pine, sweet gum, maple, oak, and dogwood. From 1937 to 1942, this seasoned company of African American World War I veterans, who earlier worked at Palmetto, Kerrville, and Abilene State Parks as well as Sweetwater Metropolitan Park, made the initial improvements to the site, including construction of the combination building, the boathouse, and the dam and spillway, following the designs of architects Paul E. Pressler, George T. Patrick, and Donald D. Obert. The spillway gave way after a 1940 flood and Lake Raven drained. While this threatened to jeopardize the overall project, work soon continued on key park elements.

Supplemental work at the park came through the efforts of two CCC forestry companies—873 and 1827—assigned there between 1933 and 1937 for firefighting and flood control in the area; they also built unpaved roads, including some on parkland. Now largely forested over, these former roads are discernible through culverts and a stone bridge along the Triple C Trail. With the advent of World War II, the CCC work ended, but WPA workers and prison laborers completed projects that included building roads and water and septic systems, allowing the park to open for limited activities during summer months of the war years. Postwar projects at the park, including reconstruction of the spillway, restoration of the lake, and development of new campsites, shelters, trails, and other amenities, serve to complement the earlier work of the CCC.

Indian Lodge

Location: Jeff Davis County, 4 miles northwest of Fort Davis, State Highway 118 to Park Road 3
Dates of CCC activity: 1933–1938, 1940–1942
CCC companies: 879, 881, and 1856
CCC construction: Indian Village Hotel (Indian Lodge), water storage reservoir, well, and pipeline.

Indian Lodge, 2009. (John B. Chandler, TPWD)

Park description: Architects J. B. Roberts, Olin Smith, Arthur Fehr, and William C. Caldwell and landscape architect Roy S. Ferguson worked on Indian Village, a sixteen-room pueblo-style hotel set on the north slope of Keesey Canyon in Davis Mountains State Park. Built of hand-hewn pine beams and adobe blocks made on-site, the hotel was adorned by longleaf-pine floors, casement windows, cane and log ceilings, hand-carved cedar furniture (built by the CCC in the shop at Bastrop State Park), and a plazalike exterior courtyard. The completed interiors and exteriors artfully recall the indigenous adobe Native American and Spanish architecture of the Southwest.

During the construction phase, CCC Companies 879 and 881 molded adobe blocks from a mixture of water, straw, and soil and muscled tens of thousands of forty-pound blocks into place to form the twelve- to eighteen-inch-thick walls, several of which rise as high as three stories. The interior made use of hand-hewn pine vigas harvested locally from Mount Livermore and river cane latilla ceilings that add to the "natural" character of the lobby. Company 1856, having already moved to Balmorhea State Park and the park camp at Big Bend, later worked at Indian Lodge as a side camp and added many features, including electrical wiring and a new roof. They also gave the lodge an initial painting to seal the portland cement plaster over the adobe-brick walls.

Almost thirty years later, in 1964–1965, TPWD built a twenty-four-room addition that included a dining room, meeting room, and swimming pool; it also "modernized" the original structure. In 2004–2006, TPWD took steps to restore the original section of the hotel to its 1935 appearance. Today Indian Lodge stands as a historically significant artifact of early automobile tourism, an example of southwestern regional romantic architecture, a model of CCC arts and crafts revival, and an illustration of a popular place to visit during the World War II years.

Inks Lake State Park

Location: Burnet County, 9 miles west of Burnet, State Highway 29 to Park Road 4
Dates of CCC activity: 1940–1942
CCC company: 854
CCC construction: Interior park roads and associated stone culverts (Park Road 4 completed by the State Highway Department in 1942), boathouse, and dock. Fireplaces, garage and compound, beach area, concession building, and custodian's dwelling were designed but not built.

Park description: With its dependable water source, abundant fish and game, and natural beauty, the region of Central Texas around the Colorado River and present Inks Lake has been an inviting location for centuries, attracting Native American, German, and Anglo settlers. In 1937, while running as a candidate for the surrounding congressional district, Lyndon Baines Johnson promised voters that he would create a "Tennessee Valley Authority–type" of transformation for the Colorado River, including dams for flood control and electricity, bridges and highways, and recreational facilities along the river. Johnson's victory soon brought into being the Lower Colorado River Authority (LCRA) and with it the benefits of rural electrification for residents of the Texas Hill Country. Shortly after Inks Lake was created by a new Colorado River dam, courtesy of the LCRA in 1938,

Inks Lake State Park, 2004. (TPWD)

Johnson sought CCC involvement to further enhance the river's comprehensive development. Having completed work at Longhorn Cavern State Park, CCC enrollees in Company 854 moved to Inks Lake and focused on constructing and supplying amenities, including the park road and recreational facilities along the lake's northern shore. The State Parks Board, the NPS, and the CCC envisioned even grander plans for Inks Lake on both shores, but the threat of World War II curtailed further projects.

Lake Brownwood State Park

Location: Brown County, 16 miles northwest of Brownwood, State Highway 279 to Park Road 15

Dates of CCC activity: 1934–1942 (1933, State Parks Board)

CCC companies: 872 and 849

CCC and other New Deal construction: Entrance portals, Park Road 15, combination building/clubhouse (built by the Civil Works Administration [CWA] and expanded by the CCC), cook's quarters, guest cottage, caretaker's house, game warden's cottage, sixteen cabins, Lookout House stairs and pier, fishermen's barracks, furnishings, bathhouse, stone boat docks, trails, trailside rests, picnic facilities, and concessionaire's residence. The concessionaire's store and service station was designed but not constructed.

Clubhouse (also combination building), Lake Brownwood State Park, ca. 1994. (TPWD)

Park description: A dam built at the confluence of Pecan Bayou and Jim Ned Creek formed Lake Brownwood, an area whose history is made rich by Native Americans, Spanish explorers, and European and Anglo-American settlers attracted to the water and attendant wildlife. In 1933, the Brown County Water Improvement District sold 537.5 acres on its new Lake Brownwood to the State Parks Board for one dollar, for the purpose of establishing a state park on the lake.

Known first as Brownwood State Park and then as Thirty-Sixth Division State Park, Lake Brownwood State Park stands, with its many structures designed by NPS architects and executed by CCC enrollees, as the most extensively developed CCC park in Texas. Begun by the CWA in 1933, the park held great promise when the CCC arrived in 1934. Construction on the more than one hundred projects continued until 1942. The CWA-built native stone refectory, designed by Waco architect Roy E. Lane (appointed in late 1934 as the first state parks architect), became the centerpiece for CCC work directed by Superintendent Nottie H. Lee (later State Parks Board executive secretary). In addition, the CCC constructed numerous lakeside and trailside features made of locally quarried rock and milled lumber.

Two trail systems connect the CCC features and structures. One parallels the bank of the lake, connects all the CCC cabins with various picnic areas and fire pits, runs past the terraced CCC boat dock, and terminates at the grand concession building. The other trail rises to a rock outcrop, again linking numerous CCC features and providing excellent overviews of the lake.

Refectory, Lake Corpus Christi State Park, ca. 2004.
(TPWD)

Lake Corpus Christi State Park

Location: San Patricio, Jim Wells, and Live Oak Counties, 4 miles southwest of Mathis, State Highway 359 to Park Road 25
Dates of CCC activity: 1934–1936
CCC company: 886
CCC construction: Refectory (currently the park headquarters) and lookout tower, Park Road 25, and bridges. Two boathouses were designed, but only one was built, and it was lost to flooding. A caretaker's compound and a bathhouse were also designed but not built. A separate caretaker's dwelling was constructed on the park but has been lost due to park expansion and realignment of roads.

Park description: Once traversed by Kawakawa and Lipan Apaches, the area is drained by the Nueces River, a disputed boundary between Texas and Mexico in the mid-nineteenth century. The river now feeds the 21,000-acre Lake Corpus Christi, which is a major source of water for the city of Corpus Christi.

In 1934, CCC Company 886 formed Camp Kleberg [*sic*], named for local Congressman and King Ranch heir Richard Mifflin Kleburg. The enrollees remained at Lake Corpus Christi until the company was transferred to Palmetto State Park in October 1936.

The highlight of the 365-acre park is the refectory. It is here that architect Olin Boese, an NPS-funded architect working for the State Parks Board, designed one of the architectural gems of the state park system. Sited above a rocky peninsula and made of cast caliche block laid in random ashlar pattern, the open-air building includes a large terrace, pavilion, and stage. The building's graceful arches and lookout tower provide a grand view of the lake, and a cast-stone staircase leads from the refectory's grounds down to trails along the lake.

Combination building, Lockhart State Park, ca. 1936. (TPWD)

Lockhart State Park

Location: Caldwell County, 4 miles south of Lockhart, US Highway 183 to FM 20 to Park Road 10

Dates of CCC activity: 1935 (1933, State Parks Board)

CCC company: 3803

CCC construction: Park Road 10, stone bridge, combination building (currently the recreation hall), residence, bathhouse pavilion, furniture (at the residence), decorative outdoor lamps and hardware, stone water storage tank, dam, trailhead steps, arched bridge, culverts, footbridges (sections replaced), well, water fountain, steps, bench, picnic tables, outdoor fireplaces, and golf course. The swimming pool is no longer in use.

Park description: With just under 264 acres of land, Lockhart State Park is small but picturesque. Set in Central Texas amid greenery of elm, oak, ash, and pecan trees, the park received federal funds. The men who worked there named their barracks Camp Colp in honor of the first, and longtime, chairman of the State Parks Board, David E. Colp, a onetime resident of Lockhart. In 1948, some years after the work was completed, the facility opened free to the public and featured a swimming pool and a golf course with an elevated first tee overlooking the area below.

The park residence, which sits on level ground, was designed by Austin architect George Walling (with partners Kirk H. Scott, R. J. Hammond, and George T. Patrick). Drawing inspiration from immigrant German architecture, the dwelling has walls of stucco and stone, some half-timbering, and an outside stairway leading to an attic door. Nearby is the swimming pool, placed close to scenic Plum Creek to make use of the area's fresh spring water supply. For the elevated bluff overlooking the surrounding countryside, architect Olin Smith of the State Parks Board's Central Design Office designed a hilltop refectory, using wood-frame construction clad in "bark-edged" cedar siding. Scattered throughout the park are picnic tables, dams, bridges, and trailheads that display the CCC's simple and rather elegant designs. Taken together, the CCC features, geography, and natural environment form a pleasing composition.

Longhorn Cavern State Park

Location: Burnet County, approximately 12 miles southwest of Burnet, US Highway 281 to Park Road 4
Dates of CCC activity: 1934–1940 (1932, State Parks Board)
CCC company: 854
CCC construction: Entrance portals, Park Road 4 and improvements to its right-of-way, culverts, cavern entrance, administration building, cabin, observation tower/water tower, picnic area, custodian's dwelling, and prototype cabin C. A double cabin and prototype cabins A and B were designed but not built.

Entrance to Longhorn Cavern, February 2011. (John B. Chandler, TPWD)

Park description: Fresh off their completed work at Blanco State Park, CCC Company 854 enrollees turned their attention to the 639-acre Longhorn Cavern State Park, beginning with the arduous task of hauling some 2.5 tons of silt, debris, and guano out of the underground, river-formed limestone cavern. Thus began an organized exploration of one of Texas' natural wonders. The enrollees mapped passageways, installed more than two miles of lighting, and made improvements to allow public access.

From sediment, limestone, and crystal formations found inside the cave, the CCC, under the direction of noted architects Samuel C. P. Vosper and George Walling, fashioned a fantastic and unique set of aboveground public facilities, including the administration building, with its dramatic silhouette, colorful materials, and Gothic arches. An observation tower, one prototype tourist cabin, and cavern entrance compound stairway were also erected, all of cut stone quarried in the park.

Recently completed concession building, Meridian State Park, ca. 1941. (TPWD)

Meridian State Park

Location: Bosque County, 3 miles southwest of Meridian, State Highway 22 to Park Road 7

Dates of CCC activity: 1933–1934

CCC company: 1827(V)

CCC construction: Entrance portal, roads, water crossing, vehicle bridge, culverts, dam, and refectory, which included the bathhouse and the pergola. The CCC-built barbecue pits are no longer in use. Picnic tables were designed but not built.

Park description: The park is located along the 98th meridian on the edge of a natural transitional zone between prairies and the Hill Country, an area historian Walter Prescott Webb referred to as part of an "institutional fault" that reached from Texas to the Dakotas. CCC Company 1827, composed of World War I veterans, developed the park using local limestone and timber, primarily oak and cedar. The NPS designs are recognizable in the impressive refectory, which features ashlar-cut stone, arched entryways, a stone chimney, beamed ceilings, an open-sided pavilion, and an overall horizontal massing that visually ties the structure to its hillside setting above Lake Bosque. The refectory, which includes restrooms, a concession area, and stone stairways, serves as a transition from the park to the lake, the key landscape feature of the site. The enrollees also constructed the rock and earthen dam across Bee Creek that impounded the lake. Credit for the park's design goes to architects and planners Paul R. Roesle, Olin Smith, E. A. Dixon, and John W. Wilder.

San Francisco de los Tejas, Mission Tejas State Park, 1967. (Herman Kelly, TxDOT)

Mission Tejas State Park

Location: Houston County, in Weches at State Highway 21 and Park Road 44
Dates of CCC activity: 1933–1935
CCC company: 888
CCC construction: Mission Tejas "replica," Park Road 44, fire towers, small dam and pond, picnic areas, trail steps, fire pits, water fountains, and pavilion. The fire towers have been removed and the pavilion reconstructed, although the fireplace remains.

Park description: From deep within the Piney Woods of East Texas, Mission Tejas State Park sought to mark the place where Spain, faced with a French entry into East Texas, asserted its claim in 1690 by founding Mission San Francisco de los Tejas (now thought to lie just west of the park). Three years later, the enterprise fell apart when the Hasinai Caddo blamed disease outbreaks on the baptismal waters and the Spaniards accused them of theft. The discovery of a Spanish cannon barrel led to the park's development near the village of Weches, where the CCC set up a reforestation camp in 1933.

The Texas Forest Service developed San Francisco Mission State Forest as a tourist attraction and commemoration of early Texas history, just in time for the Texas Centennial celebration in 1936. Those individuals involved in the project—landscape architects and foresters with CCC Company 888, a "federal forest" company—sought to evoke the memory of the historic mission by building a "commemorative replica," a horizontal log building with wood-shake roof, a petrified wood fireplace, and double-hung windows. Although the young men enrolled in Company 888 spent time learning and demonstrating forest management techniques, they also expended considerable time and energy on the site's construction projects.

When this state forest site was transferred to the State Parks Board in 1957, it was renamed Mission Tejas State Park.

Mother Neff State Park

Location: Coryell County, 16 miles west of Interstate 35 (exit 315), FM 107 to State Highway 236 to Park Road 14
Dates of CCC activity: 1934–1938
CCC company: 817
CCC and other New Deal construction: Entrance portal, park roads, culverts, recreational pavilion/tabernacle, concession building/clubhouse, caretaker's dwelling, lookout tower/water tank, pump houses, drainage system, foot trails, fences, picnic facilities, garage, and storage and tool house. Despite early terracing of the floodplain as part of the CCC work, rising water related to the unanticipated construction of Lake Belton in 1954 has threatened and inundated the facilities in recent decades, especially those in the lower stretches of the park.

Pavilion, Mother Neff State Park, 2011.
(John B. Chandler, TPWD)

Park description: Located along the Leon River bottoms on land settled by Noah and Isabella Neff, the property became the site of numerous gatherings and summer chautauquas during the family's ownership. When the couple's son, Pat Morris Neff (Pat Neff), inherited the land, he named the site in honor of his mother with the intent of developing it as a state park, as she had proposed. Pat Neff was well positioned to accomplish this, having served as governor of Texas (1921–1925), as president of Baylor University (1932–1947), and as a member of the State Parks Board (1933–1939). CCC Company 817 quarried native limestone at the site and milled local oak, elm, juniper, and cottonwood to construct the pavilion, residence, concession building, and water and observation tower from which to survey the heavily wooded terrain. When the CCC left, some features of architect Guy Newhall and landscape architect Stewart King's designs remained unfinished. Many of these were addressed in the early 1940s by a nearby young women's unit of the NYA, another New Deal agency. Closely associated with the park is the adjoining locally known Old River Road—a federally assisted secondary road built in 1939 by the Texas Highway Department—which follows the Leon River for much of its length from the west entrance of the park to FM 107.

Contrary to popular belief, Mother Neff was not the first state park. The notion most likely grew from promotions by Neff himself, who felt the family site served as inspiration for the state parks program.

Refectory, Palmetto State Park, 2008. (John B. Chandler, TPWD)

Palmetto State Park

Location: Gonzales County, 10 miles northwest of Gonzales and southeast of Luling, US Highway 183 to Park Road 11
Dates of CCC activity: 1934–1937
CCC companies: 873, 886, and 1823(CV)
CCC construction: Park Road 11, low-water crossing on the San Marcos River, water tower/storage building, refectory, and residence (currently the park headquarters), barbecue pits, picnic seating, rock pool and retention dams, rock table, culverts, concrete picnic tables, and two sets of entrance portals (one stands on private land where park extension was not realized). A lone stone chimney marks the site of original CCC camp.

Park description: Set along the San Marcos River amid a verdant Central Texas landscape of bottomland forest festooned with Spanish moss, dwarf palmettos, woody vines, and extensive marshes, Palmetto State Park exemplifies many of the harmonious-with-nature concepts so integral to the NPS and CCC's work. The building designs came from Olin Smith, an architect working for the State Parks Board but funded by NPS. Landscape architects Mason Coney and C. C. Pat Fleming helped fashion the structures and features in ways that complemented the site's distinctive natural resources. The horizontal stretch of the rock pools in the picnic area and the stone-and-wood water tower (set back from the road and almost hidden in the dense vegetation) won accolades from the NPS officials during the 1930s.

Carrying the design aim of indigenous architecture further than any other like-minded project, the remarkable native-sandstone, splayed-boulder refectory seems to grow right out of the ground. With the area's lush "tropical" vegetation and unusual wetlands in mind, architect Smith designed the sandstone to appear as if emerging from the soil to form walls, thus blurring the distinction between nature and culture. To complete the illusion, the building's first roof was thatched with palmetto fronds—reportedly cut and carried from Huntsville State Park.

Palo Duro Canyon State Park

Location: Armstrong and Randall Counties, 12 miles east of Canyon, State Highway 217 to Park Road 5
Dates of CCC activity: 1933–1937
CCC companies: 1821(V), 1828(V), 1829(V), 1824(V), 2875(C), 2876(C), and 894
CCC construction: Portal house, Park Road 5, vehicle bridges, stone and metal

Coronado Lodge (currently interpretive center), Palo Duro Canyon State Park, ca. 2000. (TPWD)

culverts, stone low-water crossings, headquarters building, Spring House (currently storage), Coronado Lodge (only partially completed by the CCC; currently the interpretive center), Well House (no longer in use), Cow Camp (four overnight cabins containing no bathrooms), three rim cabins, and picnic and camp unit groups (table, seats, fireplace, and garbage receptacle).

Park description: The rugged Palo Duro Canyon, the nation's second-largest such gorge, located in the High Plains of the Texas Panhandle, is home to one of the Lone Star State's largest state parks (some 28,978 acres). In the 1930s, seven different CCC outfits, four composed solely of veterans and two solely of young African Americans, were assigned the task of transforming a daunting geographical area—though clearly one of the state's most important scenic and natural areas—into an inviting park for guests.

Among the CCC's prime tasks was developing the more than eleven miles of road to gain access to the canyon floor, which they accomplished while also establishing strategically located lookout points, picnic areas, steps, and trails that accentuated the Lighthouse, Castle, and Capitol Peaks. Throughout the park Palo Duro's team of architects and planners took full advantage of the spectrum of picturesque scenes the landscape had to offer. Four Cow Camp cabins invite close-up views of the canyon floor; and Coronado Lodge, the large rubble stone concession building situated on the rim of the canyon, offers a spectacular view of the canyon stretching off into the horizon. Meanwhile, in one of the CCC's most inspired moves, three of the park's stone-constructed overnight cabins were set directly into the canyon's rim.

Possum Kingdom State Park

Location: Palo Pinto County, 17 miles north of Caddo on Park Road 33
Dates of CCC activity: 1941–1942
CCC company: 2888
CCC construction: Park Road 33, stone culverts, caretaker's cabin, concession stand, and septic system. Most of the original wooden picnic tables and stone fireplaces have been replaced. A floating pier with walkway was replaced in the 1950s; a frame boathouse was designed but not constructed.

Park description: The 1,528-acre Possum Kingdom State Park is located in the rugged canyon country of the Palo Pinto Mountains and Brazos River Valley in North Texas. Between 1936 and 1941, the Brazos River Conservation and Reclamation District, with federal assistance, built a dam across the river. The man for whom the dam is named, US Senator Morris Sheppard, a staunch supporter of the New Deal and a member of Congress for thirty-nine years, died just as construction was completed.

With parkland already set aside to develop recreational opportunities at this newly created lake, the project awaited a CCC company. In May 1941, CCC Company 2888 formally moved from Tyler State Park to begin the development of Possum Kingdom State Park. But when the lake suddenly filled to capacity in April 1941, the plans changed. Designers had to abandon the scheme for development along both shorelines and, instead, focused only on the west shore where the CCC gave priority to providing utilities and basic services. The enrollees cleared the park area and shoreline, built campsites and picnic tables, and constructed the more than seven miles of roads and attendant culverts. Ideas for additional improvements were set aside as World War II loomed. CCC Company 2888 finally abandoned its barracks on July 13, 1942, the last such company in Texas to do so, thus ending the CCC's impressive nine-year contribution to public works in Texas.

Tyler State Park

Location: Smith County, north of Tyler, 2 miles north of Interstate 20 on FM 14 to Park Road 16
Dates of CCC activity: 1935–1941
CCC company: 2888
CCC construction: Park Road 16, bridges, culverts, combination building and dance terrace, bathhouse, boathouse, caretaker's residence, garage, earthen dam, table and bench combinations, camp fireplaces, and diving tower.

Morris Sheppard Dam, Possum Kingdom State Park, 1997. (TPWD)

Rockwork abutments, Tyler State Park, ca. 1990. (TPWD)

Park description: Set in the Piney Woods of East Texas, Tyler State Park reflects two major park development efforts. The first, directed by landscape architect Ben R. Chambers, involved extensive forest reclamation and land rehabilitation that included tree planting, development of a road system, and construction of a dam and lake. Architect Joe C. Lair oversaw the other effort, which focused on the development of essential park buildings. Particularly noteworthy, the architect's designs represent a clear break from the NPS rustic style so often used at CCC parks, including many in Texas. Lair displayed a familiarity with the Prairie style, made popular by architect Frank Lloyd Wright, and helped to usher in a more modern style in the combination building, bathhouse, boathouse, and residence by using concrete and wood framing and emphasizing linear geometric forms. The transitional nature of Lair's work is significant because of its timing toward the end of the CCC's run of park projects in Texas.

NOTES

Preface

1. Patenaude, "The New Deal and Texas," p. 402.

Chapter 1

1. Men who joined the CCC were commonly known as "enrollees" and will be referred to as such throughout this book.

2. The some six hundred thousand acres of Big Bend State Park are not included in this 1942 figure because the following year that park became a national park. The numbers cited here of forty-eight parks and sixty thousand acres do not include historical parks and monuments.

3. Holland and Hill, *Youth in the CCC*, p. 8.

4. Although initially named Hoover Dam, it was known during most of the 1930s as Boulder Dam. After World War II, when memories of the Great Depression had receded, Congress changed its official name to Hoover Dam.

5. Franklin D. Roosevelt, *Congressional Record: Proceedings and Debates of the First Session of the Seventy-Third Congress*, vol. 77, pt. 1 (Washington, DC: US Government Printing Office, 1933), p. 650.

6. Robert L. Nettles, interview by Dan Utley, audio recording, July 13, 1994, Texas Archeological Research Laboratory, The University of Texas at Austin. Digitized tape and transcript reside at Historic Sites and Structures Program, TPWD, Austin.

7. Thomas Earl Jordan, interview by Scarlett Wirt, video recording, March 30, 2003, Historic Sites and Structures Program, TPWD, Austin.

8. Thurman, "Curricular and Instructional Program," p. 110.

9. George Payne, interview by Carolyn Bowles and Carolyn Vogel, video recording, March 30, 2003, Historic Sites and Structures Program, TPWD, Austin.

10. Utley and Steely, *Guided with a Steady Hand*, p. 15. The DRT assumed responsibility for the Alamo.

11. See Cantrell and Turner, *Lone Star Pasts*; and Buenger, *Path to a Modern South*.

12. At the time Pat Neff became governor, historical parks included the Alamo, San Jacinto, Gonzales, and Washington-on-the-Brazos State Parks; Fannin (battleground) State Park and King's State Park (Refugio); and the monuments at Acton (grave site of Davy Crockett's second wife, Elizabeth Patton Crockett) and La Grange (grave site of those who died in the Dawson and the Mier expeditions, currently operated by TPWD as Monument Hill State Historic Site).

13. Utley and Steely, *Guided with a Steady Hand*, pp. 26–32. For the influential role played by the first Parks Board chairman, the dogged David E. Colp, see also Steely, *Parks for Texas*.

14. Steely, *Parks for Texas*, p. 21.

15. Jim Cox, "Civilian Conservation Corps: Fond Memories from a Time of National Hardship," *Texas Parks & Wildlife* 36, no. 9 (September 1978): 2–7. Cox notes that the federal government had spent more than $1 million on the state park system; that figure is not confirmed.

16. Ben H. Proctor, "Great Depression," in *New Handbook of Texas*, 3:301–309.

17. James W. Steely, "Building Texas State Parks" and "Inspired by Nature," September 2008, draft text for TPWD's CCC Web site, The Look of Nature.

18. James W. Steely, interview by Michelle Williams, video recording, September 8, 2008, Historic Sites and Structures Program, TPWD, Austin.

Chapter 2

1. Alonzo Wassom, "State's Park System Given Federal Help—Conservation Corps Does Improvement Work That Would Otherwise Have Cost Millions," *Dallas Morning News*, December 10, 1933. Wassom gives 176 as the number of companies.

2. Steely, *Parks for Texas*, chap. 1.

3. Bonham State Park and Garner State Park, although Garner was said to have to be convinced by his wife to have a park named after him.

4. Otto Pruetz, interviewer unidentified, video recording, August 28, 1997, Historic Sites and Structures Program, TPWD, Austin.

5. Robert Nettles talked about his experience working at Mother Neff State Park in Utley and Steely, *Guided with a Steady Hand*, pp. 39–43.

6. Garner SP, State Parks Board records, TSLAC.

7. Joe James, interview by Janelle Taylor, Mark Thurman, Don Hudson, and Todd Imboden, video recording, July 1, 2003, Historic Sites and Structures Program, TPWD, Austin.

8. Russell Cashion, interview by David Carleton, video recording, March 30, 2003, Historic Sites and Structures Program, TPWD, Austin.

9. Lolo Baeza, interview by Janelle Taylor, video recording, June 25, 2002, Historic Sites and Structures Program, TPWD, Austin.

10. Edward Dutchover, interview by Janelle Taylor, video recording, June 25, 2002, Historic Sites and Structures Program, TPWD, Austin.

11. Gardner Hill, interview by Dennis Cordes, video recording, March 3, 2003, Historic Sites and Structures Program, TPWD, Austin.

12. James Garner, interview by Janelle Taylor and Diane Foshee, video recording, July 10, 2003, Historic Sites and Structures Program, TPWD, Austin.

13. Baeza interview.

14. James Garner, Henry Trees, and Walter Trees, group interview by Janelle Taylor and David Ham, video recording, July 10, 2003, Historic Sites and Structures Program, TPWD, Austin. The men continued, "Our blacksmith shop made all these fixtures. Every one of these light fixtures was built there in the blacksmith shop. The switch boxes and hinges, all of the iron work you see here, they built."

15. William Discher, interviewer unidentified, video recording, March 31, 2003, Historic Sites and Structures Program, TPWD, Austin.

16. Monroe Freeman, interviewer unidentified, video recording, n.d. [1998], Historic Sites and Structures Program, TPWD, Austin.

17. Ezekiel Rhodes, interview by Dale Martin and Tom Fisher, video recording, March 31, 2003, Historic Sites and Structures Program, TPWD, Austin. Former enrollees frequently referred to the CCC as the "CC Camp" or the "3 Cs."

18. Holland and Hill, *Youth in the CCC*, pp. 57–90, 235–244.

19. Utley and Steely, *Guided with a Steady Hand*, p. 72.

20. In 1933, Commissioner of the Bureau of Indian Affairs John Collier made sure that enlistment privileges were extended to Native Americans, who worked on their own reservations and did not live in camps. Collier insisted that projects on reservations should be built, maintained, and used by only Native Americans. Between 1933 and 1942, the CCC employed more than eighty thousand Native Americans.

21. Cole, *The African-American Experience*, p. 42.

22. Ibid., p. 12; Salmond, *The Civilian Conservation Corps*, pp. 88–101.

23. Dan Utley, "African-American Contributions," September 2008, draft text for TPWD's CCC Web site, The Look of Nature.

24. Cole, *The African-American Experience*, p. 4.

25. Most Native American and African American camps were segregated and were led by white officers and educational advisers. Black Americans were singled out as a group in official documents and were often treated with obvious discrimination as employees in the CCC.

26. Henry Trees, in James Garner, Henry Trees, and Walter Trees, group interview.

27. Willie D. Harris, interview by Angela Reed, video recording, July 30, 2010, Historic Sites and Structures Program, TPWD, Austin.

28. Lasswell, *Shovels and Guns*.

29. Luther Wandall, "A Negro in the CCC," *Crisis* 42 (August 1935): 4.

Chapter 3

1. "History of Texas Parks Board" (updated narrative consolidation), Joan Pearsall, June 24, 1974, with contributions by Dr. Harold Toy and Fred McNeil, p. 19. Departmental history project research files, Texas Parks and Wildlife Department administrative records and other materials, Archives and Information Services Division, Texas State Library and Archives Commission.

2. *San Antonio Evening News*, June 2, 1943.

3. Tyler State Park is one example of those parks where work was continuing as "preparedness" was ramping up. Tyler SP, State Parks Board records, TSLAC.

4. Garner SP, Texas State Parks Board records, TSLAC.

5. Possum Kingdom SP, State Parks Board records, TSLAC.

6. E. A. Pesonen, "Lure of the State Parks," *Texas Planning Bulletin Supplement* (April 1937): 40. In State Parks Board Collection, Administrative files, Texas Planning Board, *Texas Planning Bulletin* (April–December 1937), TSLAC.

7. *S-Parks* (August 1941), p. 14. The newsletter of the State Parks Board is variously referred to as *S-Parks*, *S-PARKS*, and *SPARKS*. The board's staff contributed and published it on a monthly, sometimes irregular, basis and circulated it among the staff.

8. Kerrville State Park was constructed by the CCC and is currently operated by the City of Kerrville as Kerrville-Schreiner Park.

9. Pearsall et al., "History," pp. 22–23.

10. Ibid., p. 23.

11. Ibid.

12. Toney, "The Texas State Parks System," p. 142. In 1946, the State Parks Board granted the manager of Bonham State Park the right to sub-

lease the carnival ride concession there. Bonham SP, Texas State Parks Board records, TSLAC.

13. General and Special Laws of Texas, 42nd Leg. (1931) at 287–288. See also Toney, "The Texas State Parks System," pp. 38–43. For an example of a biennial budget for the Texas State Parks Board and state parks, see General and Special Laws of Texas, 45th Leg. (1937) at 1449–1450.

14. Bentsen–Rio Grande Valley had been acquired as a state park in 1944.

15. The 77th Legislature transferred Fort Griffin to the Texas Historical Commission; the park has few CCC features.

16. By 1949, in addition to these eight historical parks, the Parks Board had acquired the seven acres at Lake Medina and six acres at Independence in 1946 and 1947, respectively. Meanwhile, several parks had been returned to donors; and Big Bend had become a national park. Only in 1965 did Fannin Battleground fall under the jurisdiction of TPWD.

17. W. R. Chambers, *Mexia News Daily*, September 3, 1945 (clipping). Fort Parker SP, State Parks Board records, TSLAC. See Toney, "The Texas State Parks System," pp. 85–87.

18. "New State Park Dedicated," *Humble Sales Lubricator* 11, no. 10 (May 8, 1941): 4. Fort Parker SP, State Parks Board records, TSLAC.

19. Toney, "The Texas State Parks System," pp. 156–157.

20. For example, a report by the Legislative Council in 1958 gave three numbers, varying between fifty-eight and sixty-one, as the total number of parks in Texas. See ibid., p. 156.

21. "Letters to the Tri-State Forum: Criticism by Visitor of Palo Duro Park Answered," *Amarillo News-Globe*, July 20, 1955 (clipping). Palo Duro Canyon SP, State Parks Board records, TSLAC.

22. Ibid.

23. Daingerfield SP, Texas State Parks Board records, TSLAC.

24. SJR 4, 55th Leg., R.S., 1957 (session laws, p. 1630), Amendments to the Texas Constitution since 1876, Research Division, Texas Legislative Council, May 2010, www.tlc.state.tx.us/pubsconamend/constamend1876 .pdf.

25. Millard Fillmore Rutherford, interview by Dale Martin and Tom Fisher, video recording, March 31, 2003, Historic Sites and Structures Program, TPWD, Austin.

26. For more on this topic, especially the case of *T. R. Register et al. v. J. D. Sandefer, Jr. et al.*, pertaining to Tyler State Park, see Toney, "The Texas State Parks System," chap. 5.

27. President Dwight D. Eisenhower signed the Federal-Aid Highway Act of 1956 into law in June of that year. Known as the National Interstate and Defense Highways Act (Pub. L. No. 84-627), it authorized $25 billion to construct more than forty thousand miles of highways over the anticipated twenty years.

28. Lonn Taylor and Joe C. Freeman, "Indian Lodge, Davis Mountains State Park, Historic Structure Report," prepared for Texas Parks and Wildlife Department (2007), pp. 26–27. Taylor cites Texas v. Espy, cause #924, Minutes of 83rd District Court (1962), Book 3 at 284–285, and notes that legislative advocacy allowed funding sufficient to enlarge the lodge.

29. *Texas House Journal*, 58th Leg., Regular Session (1963) at 71. Although the report was published after Connally's pronouncement, the long-standing funding needs of state parks had been widely acknowledged.

30. However, the executive director of the Game and Fish Commission, who had failed to fire the offending warden, was not chosen as the new department's leader.

31. Mike Herring, "Texas State Parks History," unpublished manuscript, updated March 2011, p. 3.

32. Ibid., p. 5.

33. Bob Armstrong, telephone conversation with Brandimarte, January 15, 2011.

34. John Jefferson, "The Golden Age of Park Acquisitions," *Texas Parks & Wildlife* 69, no. 8 (August 2011): 22–29. Jefferson mentions some of the sixty-three parks, historic sites, and state natural areas that TPWD acquired from 1963 until 1988.

Chapter 4

1. James Wright Steely, interview by Michelle Williams, Bastrop State Park, video recording, September 8, 2008, Historic Sites and Structures Program, TPWD, Austin. On the legacy of the CCC parks, see also Steely, *Parks for Texas*, pp. 194–195.

2. Sue Moss, telephone conversation with Brandimarte, January 5, 2012.

3. The centennial of the CCC will occur in 2033, and that of the Texas State Parks Board in 2023.

4. The exhibit was produced in April 1986. Moss planned and wrote the text, and contract artist John Ianelli designed the exhibit in conjunction with TPWD's Exhibit Shop. James Wright Steely authored the accompanying booklet; his research became the basis for his later writing on the CCC. The booklet was updated and redesigned by TPWD in conjunction with the original author in 2010.

5. In the regions, TPWD natural and cultural resources programs have conservation biologists and archeologists on staff. The Archeology Survey Team is led by Margaret Howard, Aina Dodge, Logan McNatt, Luis Alvarado, and Joshua Gibbs.

6. TPWD has had the good fortune to work with a number of gifted historians, architectural historians, and architects on CCC-park studies: Terri Myers on Fort Parker, 1996; Diane E. Williams on Lake Brownwood, 1996; Julie Strong on Garner, 1996, and Goliad, 1997; Lila Knight on Bastrop with Ralph Newlan, 1994, Balmorhea, 1996, and Tyler, 1997.

Throughout the 1990s, Dan Utley wrote the historical sections included in a number of brief archeological reports for Abilene, Daingerfield, and Meridian State Parks. More recently, Martha Doty Freeman prepared a cultural landscape report on Abilene, and Diane E. Williams completed architectural inventories of Balmorhea, Huntsville, Blanco, and Mission Tejas. In preparation for the rehabilitation of Indian Lodge, historian Lonn Taylor and architect Joe Freeman co-authored a historic structures report on that facility. Under the direction of historic architect Dennis Gerow, the following architectural firms authored condition assessments of CCC parks: Limbacher & Godfrey Architects; Joe Freeman, Architect; Halff Associates, Inc.; and Quimby McCoy Preservation Architecture, LLP.

7. Although the National Register has always accepted and listed historic districts as eligible properties, with the category "district" spelled out in the original National Register regulations, the majority of listings early on were for single properties. With the establishment of the historic tax credits and other financial incentives and preservation programs, there was an increase in the development of district nominations in the 1980s and 1990s. "As the number of unidentified individual gems has decreased, more and more historic districts become the best mechanism for listing," says Paul Lusignan, historian, National Register of Historic Places, NPS. Lusignan, e-mail to Cynthia Brandimarte, March 8, 2012.

8. Interpretive Services staff has recently completed a CCC Photo Safari that encourages visitors to CCC parks to locate and photograph selected CCC features. Among the interpreters who work on regional projects are Linda Hedges, Walt Bailey, Ben Horstmann, Barbara Parmley, Karen Watson, and Tara Humphreys; the staff also includes Sally Baulch-Rhoden, Joanne Avant, Dana Younger, and Chris Holmes, as well as site interpreters.

9. Ethan Carr, National Historic Landmark Nomination, Bastrop State Park, 1995.

Epilogue

1. Company 1805 had transferred to Wyoming by April 1937; Company 1811 stayed at Bastrop-Buescher until October 1939.

2. "Brush Fire Put Out by CCC Boys" (clipping). Bastrop SP, State Parks Board records, TSLAC.

3. Jeff Sparks, interview by Cynthia Brandimarte, video recording, September 28, 2011, Historic Sites and Structures, Program, TPWD, Austin.

4. Ibid.

5. Robert Crossman, interview by Cynthia Brandimarte, video recording, October 4, 2011, Historic Sites and Structures, Program, TPWD, Austin.

6. Ibid.

7. Ibid.

8. Sparks interview.

9. Crossman interview.

10. Ibid.

11. Sparks interview.

12. Crossman interview.

13. David Riskind, interview by Cynthia Brandimarte, video recording, October 4, 2011, Historic Sites and Structures, Program, TPWD, Austin.

14. Todd McClanahan, e-mail to Angela Reed, January 2, 2012.

BIBLIOGRAPHY

The most valuable sources for this book were the Texas State Parks Board Records and Texas Parks and Wildlife Department records housed at the Texas State Library and Archives Commission. The board records document the development and maintenance of the state park system in Texas by the Texas State Parks Board and the work of the board with the Civilian Conservation Corps, the Work Projects Administration, and other federal agencies at individual state parks and statewide. There are varied types of records that generally cover 1901–1963, with the bulk dating 1933–1949. TPWD records document the agency's responsibility for the management and conservation of the state's natural and cultural resources, provision of outdoor recreational opportunities, conservation education and outreach, and interpretation of cultural and historical resources. The varied record types cover 1963–1999 with a few earlier records. The history project files document the early years of the TPWD (1963–1975) and were especially helpful. Please consult www.tsl.state.tx.us for an online inventory of these catalogued collections, as well as the scans of the original CCC drawings.

The Historic Sites and Structures Program files include photocopied records from Record Group 79 from the National Archives and Records Administration, Denver, Colorado. Collected during 2004 and 2005 research trips to Denver, the files contain NPS records about Texas' CCC parks. Program files also contain microfiche of available Texas CCC camp newspapers and microfilm of available Texas CCC camp newspapers and *Happy Days*, the national CCC newspaper.

TPWD In-House and Contracted Studies

Brandimarte, Cynthia, and Lila Knight. "History of the Balmorhea Area and Balmorhea State Park." 1996.

Carpenter, Stephen M., and Dan K. Utley. "Dust on the Water: The Cultural Resources of Daingerfield State Park." 1996.

Drake, Douglas, Dan K. Utley, and Carole A. Medlar. "Archeological Survey of a 320-Acre Tract in Inks Lake State Park, Burnet County, Texas." 1996.

Freeman, Martha Doty. "Abilene State Park: A History of the Development of a Cultural Landscape, 1875–2003." 2003.

Hammons, Carlyn Copeland. "A Guide to TPWD's CCC Oral History Interview Collection." 2004.

Kinslow, Jack. "Music of CCC-Era Texas." 2005.

Kinslow, Jack, and Allison Ewing. "A Guide to TPWD's CCC Oral History Interview Collection, Volume 2." 2005.

Knight, Lila, for Ralph Edward Newlan, Historic Preservation Consultant. "Tyler State Park, Smith County, Texas, Cultural Resources Survey Report." 1995.

Mace, Erin. "Interview with Raiford Stripling (1910–1990), Restoration Architect." 2006.

Medlar, Carole A., Dan K. Utley, and S. Christopher Caran. "Texas Central: The Cultural Resources of Meridian State Park, Bosque County, Texas." 1996.

Myers, Terri, with Diana Nicklaus, for Hardy, Heck, Moore & Associates, Inc. "Historic Narrative and Cultural Resources Survey: Fort Parker State Park." 1993.

Newlan, Ralph Edward. "Bastrop State Park: Bastrop, Texas, Cultural Resources Survey Report." 1993.

Steely, James Wright. "The Civilian Conservation Corps in Texas State Parks." Brochure produced for Texas Parks and Wildlife Department, August 1986. 2010.

Strong, Julie W. "A History of Garner State Park." 1996.

———. "A History of Goliad State Park and Historic Site." 1997.

Turpin, Jeff, Dan K. Utley, and S. Chris Caran. "Where the Buffalo Roamed: Cultural Resources of Abilene State Park, Taylor County." 1997.

Utley, Dan K., Stephen M. Carpenter, S. Chris Caran, and Solveig A. Turpin. "Mother Neff State Park: Prehistory, Parks, and Politics, Coryell County, Texas." 1996.

Williams, Diane E. "Historic Resources Survey and Narrative History, Lake Brownwood State Park, Brown County, Texas." 1997.

———. "Historic Resources Survey, Brief Narrative and Report, Blanco Sate Park." 2008.

———. "Historic Resources Survey, Narrative History and Report, Balmorhea State Park, Reeves County, Texas." 2010.

———. "Historic Resources Survey, Narrative History and Report, Huntsville State Park, Walker County, Texas." 2009.

———. "Historic Resources Survey, Narrative History, Historic Landscape Assessment and Report, Mission Tejas State Park." 2011.

Architectural References

Carr, Ethan. *Wilderness by Design: Landscape Architecture & the National Park Service.* Lincoln: University of Nebraska Press, 1998.

Cutler, Phoebe. *The Public Landscape of the New Deal.* New Haven, CT: Yale University Press, 1985.

Good, Albert H. *Park and Recreation Structures: Administration and Basic Service Facilities; Recreational and Cultural Facilities; Overnight and Organized Camp.* 1938. Repr., New York: Princeton Architectural Press, 1999.

———. *Patterns from the Golden Age of Rustic Design: Park and Recreation Structures from the 1930's.* Lanham, MD: Roberts Rinehart Publishers, 2003.

McClelland, Linda Flint. *Building the National Parks: Historic Landscape Design and Construction.* Baltimore: Johns Hopkins University Press, 1998.

———. *Presenting Nature: The Historic Landscape Design of the National Park Service, 1916–1942.* Washington, DC: National Park Service, 1993.

Histories of the Era

Alter, Jonathan. *The Defining Moment: FDR's Hundred Days and the Triumph of Hope.* New York: Simon and Schuster Paperbacks, 2007.

Brands, H. W. *Traitor to His Class: The Privileged Life and Radical Presidency of Franklin Delano Roosevelt.* New York: Doubleday, 2008.

Buenger, Walter L. *The Path to a Modern South: Northeast Texas between Reconstruction and the Great Depression.* Austin: University of Texas Press, 2001.

Cantrell, Gregg, and Elizabeth Hayes Turner. *Lone Star Pasts: Memory and History in Texas.* College Station: Texas A&M University Press, 2006.

Cohen, Robert. *Dear Mrs. Roosevelt: Letters from Children of the Great Depression.* Chapel Hill: University of North Carolina Press, 2002.

Egan, Timothy. *The Worst Hard Time: The Untold Story of Those Who Survived the Great American Dust Bowl.* New York: Houghton Mifflin, 2006.

Hurt, R. Douglas. *The Dust Bowl: An Agricultural and Social History.* Chicago: Nelson-Hall, 1981.

Lange, Howard L. *The CCC: A Humanitarian Endeavor during the Great Depression.* New York: Vantage Press, 1984.

Shogan, Robert. *Backlash: The Killing of the New Deal.* Chicago: Ivan R. Dee, 2006.

Sterner, Richard. *The Negro's Share.* New York: Harper and Brothers Publishers, 1943.

Watkins, T. H. *The Great Depression: America in the 1930s.* Boston: Little, Brown, 1993.

Worster, Donald. *Dust Bowl: The Southern Plains in the 1930s.* New York: Oxford University Press, 1979.

Histories of the CCC

Butler, Ovid, ed. *Youth Rebuilds: Stories for the C.C.C.* Washington, DC: American Forestry Association, 1934.

Cole, Olen, Jr. *The African-American Experience in the Civilian Conservation Corps.* Gainesville: University Press of Florida, 1999.

Cornebise, Alfred E. *The CCC Chronicles: Camp Newspapers of the Civilian Conservation Corps, 1933–1942.* Jefferson, NC: McFarland, 2004.

Dearborn, Ned H. *Once in a Lifetime: A Guide to the CCC Camp.* New York: Charles E. Merrill, 1936.

Harper, Charles Price. *The Administration of the Civilian Conservation Corps.* Clarksburg, WV: Clarksburg Publishing, 1939.

Hendrickson, Kenneth E., Jr. "The Civilian Conservation Corps in the Southwestern States." In *The Depression in the Southwest*, edited by Donald W. Whisenhunt, pp. 3–25. Port Washington, NY: Kennikat Press, 1980.

———. "Replenishing the Soil and the Soul of Texas: The CCC in the Lone Star State as an Example of State-Federal Work Relief during the Great Depression." *Faculty Papers of Midwestern University* 1, ser. 2 (1974–1975): 37–48.

Holland, Kenneth, and Frank Ernest Hill. *Youth in the CCC.* Washington, DC: American Council on Education, 1942.

Johnson, Charles W. "The Army and the Civilian Conservation Corps, 1933–42." In *Prologue: The Journal of the National Archives*, pp. 139–156. Washington DC: National Archives and Records Service, 1972.

———. "The Civilian Conservation Corps: The Role of the Army." PhD diss., University of Michigan, 1968.

Lasswell, James. *Shovels and Guns: The CCC in Action.* New York: International Pamphlets, 1935.

McEntee, James J. *Now They Are Men: The Story of the CCC.* Washington, DC: National Home Library Foundation, 1940.

New Handbook of Texas. 6 vols. Austin: Texas State Historical Association, 1996.

Patenaude, Lionel V. "The New Deal and Texas." PhD diss., University of Texas at Austin, 1953.

Salmond, John. *The Civilian Conservation Corps, 1933–1942: A New Deal Case Study.* Durham, NC: Duke University Press, 1967.

Stallings, Frank L., Jr. *Black Sunday: The Great Dust Storm of April 14, 1935.* Austin: Eakin Press, 2001.

Steely, James Wright. *Parks for Texas: Enduring Landscapes of the New Deal.* Austin: University of Texas Press, 1999.

Sypolt, Larry N. *Civilian Conservation Corps: A Selectively Annotated Bibliography.* Westport, CT: Praeger Publishers, 2005.

Thonhoff, Robert H. *Camp Kenedy, Texas.* Austin: Eakin Press, 2003.

Thurman, Claude Harrison. "The Curricular and Instructional Program of the Junior White Civilian Conservation Corps Camps of the North and South Texas Districts." PhD diss., University of Texas at Austin, 1940.

Toney, Sharon Morris. "The Texas State Parks System: An Administrative History, 1923–1984." PhD diss., Texas Tech University, 1995.

Utley, Dan K., and James W. Steely. *Guided with a Steady Hand: The Cultural Landscape of a Rural Texas Park.* Waco: Baylor University Press, 1998.

Walker, Helen M. *The CCC through the Eyes of 272 Boys: A Summary of a Group Study of the Reactions of 272 Cleveland Boys to Their Experience in the Civilian Conservation Corps.* Cleveland, OH: Western Reserve University Press, 1938.

Wirth, Conrad L. *Parks, Politics, and the People.* Norman: University of Oklahoma Press, 1980.

Pictorial Histories and Reminiscences of the CCC

Cohen, Stan. *The Tree Army: A Pictorial History of the Civilian Conservation Corps, 1933–1942.* Missoula, MT: Pictorial Histories Publishing, 1980.

Cox, Thomas R. *The Park Builders: A History of State Parks in the Pacific Northwest.* Seattle: University of Washington Press, 1988.

Davis, Frank C. *My C.C.C. Days: Memories of the Civilian Conservation Corps.* Boone, NC: Parkway Publishers, 2006.

Engbeck, Joseph H., Jr. *By the People, for the People: The Work of the Civilian Conservation Corps in California State Parks, 1933–1941.* State of California: Sacramento: California State Parks, 2002.

Hayden, Ernest A. *The United States Civilian Conservation Corps of the 1930's.* Callahan, CA: Ernst A. Hayden, 1985.

Hill, Edwin G. *In the Shadow of the Mountain: The Spirit of the CCC.* Pullman: Washington State University Press, 1990.

Howell, Glenn. *CCC Boys Remember: A Pictorial History of the CCC.* Medford, OR: Klocker Printery, 1976.

Kiefer, E. Kay, and Paul E. Fellows. *Hobnail Boots and Khaki Suits: A Brief Look at the Great Depression and the Civilian Conservation Corps as Seen through the Eyes of Those Who Were There.* Chicago: Adams Press, 1983.

Lacy, Leslie Alexander. *The Soil Soldiers: The Civilian Conservation Corps in the Great Depression.* Radnor, PA: Chilton, 1976.

Merrill, Perry H. *Roosevelt's Forest Army: A History of the Civilian Conservation Corps, 1933–1942.* Montpelier, VT: Self-published, 1981.

Nolte, M. Chester, ed. *Civilian Conservation Corps: The Way We Remember It, 1933–1942.* Paducah, KY: Turner Publishing, 1990.

Ryan, J. C. *The CCC and Me.* Duluth, MN: J. C. Ryan, 1987.

Sommer, Barbara W. *Hard Work and a Good Deal: The Civilian Conservation Corps in Minnesota.* St. Paul: Minnesota Historical Society Press, 2008.

Relevant Web Sites

PBS. *Surviving the Dust Bowl.* 2011. www.pbs.org/wgbh/amex/dustbowl.

Texas Parks and Wildlife Department. "Civilian Conservation Corps Legacy Parks." www.texasstateparks.org/ccc.

Texas State Library. "To Love the Beautiful: The Story of Texas State Parks." Online exhibit. February 2007. www.tsl.state.tx.us/exhibits/parks.

Wessels Living History Farm. "Farming in the 1930s." www.livinghistoryfarm.org/farminginthe30s/farminginthe1930s.html.

Wind Erosion Research Unit. "Dust Bowl References." www.weru.ksu.edu/new_weru/multimedia/dustbowl/DBReferences.html; www.weru.ksu.edu/new_weru/multimedia/multimedia.html.

INDEX